Living*with* Gusto

Elizabeth Day

Blue Root Press

Also by Elizabeth Day:

Notes from Gusto: Relationship Reminders
Notes from Gusto: Break Free

Design by Sarah Tregay, DesignWorks Creative

For Zoë and Indio

gusto

(from *Merriam-Webster Dictionary*)

pronounced **gus´**-toe

1. an individual or special taste
2. enthusiastic and vigorous enjoyment or appreciation
3. vitality marked by an abundance of vigor and enthusiasm

* * *

Gusto

pronounced **goose´**-toe

1. Ophelia's gusto

1. Who I Am

My name is Ophelia. My first instinct is to tell you that I wasn't always like this, that I changed along the way, but I've learned to tell the truth, and the truth is: this is who I've always been.

There are other truths you should know from the start: My husband is a good man. My daughter wasn't to blame either.

When a small thread hangs out of place, and you begin to pull at it, you can't put it back. It becomes a single thread pulled. You can't force it inside, tuck it between a fold, or hide it within other threads that are still intact. It will always come loose. It wants to be seen as it truly is: barely hanging on.

I was the one who pulled the final thread. It changed everything. That was the problem.

I didn't change. That was eventually the solution.

2. The Departure

I reached into the top cabinet above the kitchen sink, pulled out the nearest vase, and wiped the dust off with a paper towel. *Seven pennies in the bottom of the vase,* the florist had said—an Asian woman, significantly shorter than me with wiry, gray hair. Though she looked to be in her seventies, her intense stare and the fact that she didn't smile once made her seem ancient. Something about the effect of copper in the water, she had calmly explained, though she seemed to be mouthing something about iron in my veins. She could see right through me; of that I was sure.

In the kitchen, I emptied the small jar of change on the counter and found seven pennies. After counting them twice, I dropped them in the bottom of the vase one at a time. Just as my hand reached the faucet handle, I remembered that she had also suggested cutting a quarter of an inch off the bottom of the stems before placing them in water. *Scissors.* She had specifically said I'd need them. I went to the kitchen drawer that held everything random and rummaged through until I found a pair. Intent on following the florist's instructions so the tulips would last as long as possible, I took the cellophane wrapper off and methodically cut each stem.

Water. Before the pores in the stems close themselves off. Back to the sink. I filled the vase with a mixture of hot and cold water, first more of one, then more of the other, then dumping it out and starting all over again, until finally it was warm—not too much energy-sapping hot water and not too much shocking cold. After gently placing each of the tulips in the vase, I stared at them for a moment, probably more—though now my sense of time seems to have folded in on itself. I remember taking in the simple beauty of those tulips and feeling the same determination that had prompted me to stop and buy flowers on my way home: I wanted to witness something vividly alive.

Perhaps it innocently slipped through my hands. Or maybe I purposely dropped the vase. My guess is the latter. What I do know is that somewhere in the time it took me to take a few short steps from the sink to the kitchen table where I planned to place the vase, I found myself kneeling on the floor in a puddle of water, surrounded by broken glass and tulips I was sure were already wilting. I wanted to let the tears well up and then flow freely, but there was no reservoir left inside me. I remember thinking, *Is it possible to run out of tears? How long will it take until they fill up so I can release them again?*

And then, the puddle I was kneeling in. The broken glass. And the only words I knew were true: *I want to feel—something, anything other than what I've been feeling.*

I reached for the piece of glass resting on a petal. Pulled my hand back. Stared at the petal beneath it. Orange. The color of my blood; it couldn't possibly be red anymore. It had to have faded—lifeless as I knew I was. Then reached for the piece of glass again. Picked it up, my hand trembling.

"Oh, my Ophelia… this is not the way."

I ignored his voice and held the glass above the palm of my other hand. I could imagine it—the sharp glass piercing my skin and releasing the feelings I no longer wanted to feel, finally allowing them to spill out. Letting them flow around me like the water I was kneeling in.

"I understand, Ophelia. I promise you I do. But this isn't the way. Let me show you what you've forgotten."

I closed my eyes, unable to create an opening, yet not willing to put the glass down.

"It's time now. Come back, Ophelia."

Whispers: *Show me, Gusto. Show me. Show me. Showmeshowme…* The piece of glass fell to the floor. Then, unable to release the feelings inside me, I allowed them to swallow me. Felt myself pull back away from my body, further and further back until I could see myself kneeling there on the kitchen floor, my head in my hands, my body rocking back and forth.

"Let go and come with me. Let go, Ophelia. Surrender to it. We're almost there… I'll show you…"

3. Before the Departure

My husband and I had finished shooting a wedding together on the island of Bali. I couldn't imagine a setting more idyllic—more romantic—than Pura Tanah Lot, an old temple carved into a huge rock jutting out of the water, just offshore. When I first saw it, it reminded me of those pots housing a perfectly thriving bonsai tree, one that's surrounded by Zen rock, dotted with carved steps in stone and brilliant green moss. Serenity contained. Or so it seemed.

More than a third of the rock that made up Pura Tanah Lot was artificial, placed and made to look authentic during restoration endeavors. We found this out from our local guide, a boy of about sixteen. "Much of it is fake." He said it so casually. He also told us about rumors of venomous snakes in the waters around the base of the temple rock, meant to keep evil spirits away.

He wasn't casual about that. "Please. Be careful," he told us. "Sometimes a legend is not just a legend."

As he showed us the different spots that were best for taking pictures at different times of the day, he asked us if we had ever been to Pura Tanah Lot before, for any other occasion.

"No," my husband said. He explained how, as photographers, we often traveled to shoot destination weddings, and it sometimes took us to places we had never been.

"And the couple whose wedding you are here to take photos of. Have they been here before?"

My husband looked at me. I shrugged. "We don't know," he said. "We only met them recently, back in the States. I never asked, so I'm not sure."

"Let us hope not," the guide said.

"Why?" I asked.

"Another legend has it that if you come here with your lover before you are married, the relationship will split as decisively as the temple itself did—before it was restored."

There are no coincidences.

* * *

Since our return home after the wedding, my husband had spent most of his waking moments in our home office, browsing through the thousands of different shots, choosing which ones would make it into the final collection, and beginning the long process of editing the photos.

We were known not just for the quality of our photos, our professionalism while shooting, and the unusual candid shots we captured; we were obsessively punctual. If the photos were promised a week after the event, they would be delivered in fewer than seven days. No exceptions.

In the forty-eight hours since our return, I had found excuse after excuse not to help him, but he didn't seem to notice. When he got into the editing mode, the music played loudly, and it was like the notes were directing him. His fingertips on the keyboard, adding a brush stroke here, altering the lighting there, dropping red or purple or yellow in over there—his fingertips danced to the beat of the music. He and the photographs and the people in them and the music with its blend of loud and soft, of light and dark, they all became one.

While he was sifting through and fixing the photos, I distracted myself with to-do lists that required leaving home, even though I knew I couldn't put off the inevitable—that at some point, my husband would walk out of our office, look at me in a way he never had before, and everything would change.

4. The Arrival

"Gusto?"

"I'm here," he said.

I opened my eyes and turned. Gusto was standing by my side. "Am I dead?"

He shook his head. "No…"

"Where are we?"

Gusto looked around and then back at me as if it were more than obvious.

Before I could try to remember where I had just come from or give any thought to how I had gotten to an island I had only imagined—with someone who, from the time I was a child, I thought was just a figment of my imagination—Gusto said, "Not now. Not for now. Listen to the waves… they're greeting us." He turned his attention to the waves building and crashing before us and then waved his arms high in the air, greeting the ocean as if he had found a long-lost friend.

He pointed at the sky. "Look!"

As the sun shifted between the clouds, it looked like it was orchestrating a fashion show, quickly throwing off one outfit so the ocean could don another. Each time it peeked through the clouds, it changed the color of the ocean—its model—first from a heavy blue to a light green, then to a sleepy navy, and finally to a bright aqua.

Squinting up at the sun with his hands shielding his eyes, Gusto said, "You know what I think? It wants a dance." He nodded. "Yes, I'm sure of it."

"It feels like a welcome," I said.

"Yes. A welcome back," he said, still transfixed by the sun, which seemed to be taking on a personality right before my eyes.

Looking at the way the sun seemed to deliberately make the ocean sparkle, I thought about how whenever Gusto came into my thoughts as a child, and then even into my teenage years, he always showed up with an unabashed enthusiasm for things I would have otherwise barely noticed. As I grew older, I began to understand him as a personality that could never be contained. His presence extended so far beyond himself and was too expansive to ever pull in or close up in any way. It felt so good to be with him now, and as I watched him oblivious to everything but the sun—which had started darting in and out of the clouds again—and saw him put his hands on his hips and then take a step to the right, then to the left, to the right, to the left, I found myself smiling. He was ridiculous; he knew it, and I knew it, and he couldn't have cared less. All that mattered to him in that moment was his private tango with, as he put it, that "spunky ball of fire."

I decided to follow Gusto's lead and let our surroundings absorb me. I took in the few pipers scurrying across the sand, and beyond them, the long stretch of pristine beach. Reaching down, I picked up a handful of sand to make sure it was real, to confirm that I was actually standing there. Sand-carpeted pathways stretched to the east and west, and behind us, a dense jungle marked by a thick border of palms, cacti, and birds of paradise cradled the beach. No doubt about it, it was the island I had imagined since I was a child—Gusto's island, the faraway place his voice always seemed to be coming from.

When Gusto was done tangoing, he said, "My Ophelia, let's lighten up and live it up! When was the last time you had fun?"

Without waiting for an answer, he motioned for me to follow him as he turned and headed toward the jungle.

I kicked off my flip-flops and walked with Gusto—though his "walk" had a definite skip to it. Loving the warmth and softness of the flour-like sand beneath my feet, I stayed aware of that comforting contact with each step.

"Maybe you've forgotten the matter of fun," he said as we approached the nearly distinct line where the beach met the jungle.

"It feels like it's been a long time… I think it might have been," I said.

"Yes. But now. Here we are!" He turned to me and whispered in my ear: "Thank you, my Ophelia. Thank you, thank you, thank you." He looked into my eyes for a long moment and smiled. I didn't know what he was thanking me for, but the love with which he said those words was plenty enough for me to try to absorb.

As we made our way through the jungle, Gusto stopped now and then to inspect a spot on the trail, wrap his arms around a moss-covered tree trunk, and focus his attention on the fluttering wings of a hovering butterfly. Between intermittent whistling, Gusto chattered away, mostly to himself. I followed a few feet behind him, thrilled not to have to think, just to be led. Though I had a strong urge to reach forward and touch Gusto, I was afraid even the softest touch would shatter the illusion and make him disappear. And I was afraid that, for some reason, I would disappear with him.

As we moved deeper into the tangled trees and lush vegetation, Gusto started picking up long, green leaves and wide, flat palm branches that spread into our path. When his arms were full, he led me to a cluster of mango trees a short distance ahead.

While I organized and piled everything Gusto had picked up along the way, he reached up and pulled two mangos from a branch. Then he took out his pocketknife, started peeling away the skin, and told me to relax and come sit next to him. I loved watching him work with each mango, an artist absorbed in the smallest details. He paused sculpting, leaned forward with a brewing excitement, and said, "You remember who I am, Ophelia. Yes?"

I took in the sight of Gusto before me—his signature hat, his rolled-up, brown pants, and his white shirt—untucked and unbuttoned. A mango in one hand, his carving knife in the other. The sparkle in his eyes and the fullness of his presence. I said, "Yes, but tell me again." It felt like it had been years since I had last asked him to remind me.

He put down the mango and knife and said, "Feel your pulse... that's me. I'm your gusto—your zest and your zing. I'm the background music only you can hear. The part of you that loves without fear, that trusts without doubt, that's optimistic without caution. Yes, all the things people warn you about. That's who your Gusto is. The part of you that believes in everything impossible, and the part that wants to take down every wall and break out of every cage. My Ophelia, your Gusto knows with no doubts that life is delicious and beautiful and that you're meant to taste it in its fullness.

"And so I'll always ask you the questions you must ask yourself...

"What do you want, Ophelia?

"What do you need?"

A strange, foggy numbness washed over and through me, and so rather than answering, I said the only thing I was certain of in that moment. "I love your song."

He nodded and picked up where he had left off with his sculpting. After peeling the last mango, he handed it to me and said, "To the taste of life!" As he slowly brought his mango up to his mouth, his eyes were wide with what I thought might be exaggerated anticipation.

One bite, however, and I understood his excitement. I had never tasted a mango as delicious in my life. I ate it like an apple, the smooth yellow juices running down my hands and then dripping off my elbows. Gusto was obviously enjoying every bite as well. He took his time, savoring the taste, loving every minute of it, once in a while talking to himself—or the mango—I couldn't tell which.

One thing I had come to expect from Gusto, back when I had felt his presence in my everyday life—especially as a child—was that he followed his whims without explanation. So I wasn't surprised when, after we finished the mangos, Gusto pulled the brim of his hat down over his eyes, leaned back against the sprawling trunk of the tree, and went to sleep. He looked so relaxed as he slid right into the land of dreams—inviting enough that I decided to join him.

* * *

When I woke up, Gusto was whistling again, busily weaving together the branches and leaves he had picked up along the way. I suspected he had been awake for a while because the palms and lengthy leaves had been sliced into long strips. A few minutes later, his handiwork started to take form, and shortly after, he was pulling the final strand through a round-topped, wide-brimmed hat.

Holding his work proudly in front of him, he admired his creation and then turned to me and crowned my head with the woven hat.

"Do you know which one you're wearing?" he asked.

He could tell by the look on my face that I didn't understand.

"It's the unhappy hat," he explained. "You don't always recognize it, but sometimes you step back and look from a place far away." He winked. "That's when you see it."

He adjusted the hat on my head. "Sometimes it's a must to get mad. And sometimes you just don't have it in you to feel anything but stale. That's not just okay. It's delicious. Because there's nothing simple about you! And life affects you.

"My Ophelia, you can feel however you want to feel. Whenever you want to. But then, sometimes, when you've dropped into unhappiness for so long, it's hard to remember that you have a choice to feel something else when you're ready to. That you always have choices."

I still had no idea what he was talking about.

Gusto looked at me for a long moment and then said, "You don't remember, do you?"

I didn't like the sound of that. "No, not really," I said.

The sadness in Gusto's eyes sent a jolt of nervousness through me.

"Gusto? What is it?"

He looked at me and held a silence that made my heart pound.

"Gusto—say something…"

He closed his eyes, took a long, deep breath, and then slowly—ever so slowly—exhaled. With his hands on his heart, he opened his eyes and looked into mine, further than anyone had ever looked, deeper into me than I had ever gone myself. I felt his heart pumping the blood through mine, giving it its beat. That's when the dam holding back the memory of what led up to my arrival on the island broke.

All the feelings came flooding back: Wishing I could pinpoint where the emptiness in me was coming from, what was causing it. Wishing I could place my finger on a certain aspect of my life—to assign anything concrete as the problem. Wishing I knew how to fix the brokenness inside me. Wishing I could jolt the flat line I was living into one that rose higher and higher, even if only just little by little.

All I knew was that I was existing instead of thriving. Why did I feel like I was faking something too often? Why was I constantly evaluating my level of happiness, rating it on a hundred different scales, instead of just being happy? I was fine when I was busy, active, moving… but then in the quiet moments, in the shower with the water running over my face, or with my hand poised in the air while chopping vegetables, or driving with the radio turned off… that's when I felt it. Something pulling at me from the inside. And even deeper than that, an urge for more, an overwhelming desire to be more of who I was and less of who I was being, so strong that I thought more than once of walking out the door, getting on a train or a bus to somewhere I had never been, just because, just to experience it, to bring out a part of me that was dormant, or—I feared more than anything else—had never really existed.

I remembered now… Wanting to make myself hollow so I could start all over and fill up with new things that made me feel alive again, experiences and people that brought out the parts of me that were the corners of the puzzle, the inside pieces, the border—not just the picture on the cover of the box. The emptiness inside me was so overwhelming and the feelings about myself and my life so heavily negative, I wanted to pierce my skin to just release it all, to let it flow out.

The piece of broken glass in my hand, dangling in the air. Unable to move forward, refusing to move backwards. The weight of meaninglessness bearing down on me until I finally curled up beneath it and begged, *Show me, show me, show me,* until it blended into *showmeshowmeshowme.* I didn't even know what I wanted shown to me. They were simply the only words that made sense to beg.

Staring at Gusto now, I swallowed hard, trying to hold back my emotions, until a part of me felt overwhelmingly grateful for the ability to cry. I let the tears find their way out, one after another until I could barely catch my breath.

"I'm pathetic," I sobbed. "There's no excuse. I'm so sorry, I'm so sorry, Gusto… how could I get to that point?"

Gusto placed his hands on my cheeks and gently lifted my face toward him. He was real—or at least as real as I was. I knew in that moment as his hands cradled my face. "Let your tears come. All of them. I'm not going anywhere, because I know you, my Ophelia. I know you."

"I don't know who I am anymore," I said, pleading for him to tell me.

Gusto's eyes sparkled, and his smile pulled me right into his words. "You're someone who's so in love with life—but you haven't been in love with *your* life for a long time. That's all. Just a little separation there."

I nodded, the pieces starting to come together from the distant perspective. *I wanted to be shown how to live again…*

"Yes. Your life has become like many flat lines. No oomph. No real cares—things you really care about. Your passion has been buried inside you, under layers and layers of shoulds and should-nots, instead of reaching out from you. And believe me, it doesn't just want to peek out from you, it wants to take you by the hand and lead the way. Oh yes, my Ophelia—your passion has a mind of its own."

He pointed at my heart and said, "You have so much happening inside you… always."

I could feel it. Movement. A speck of sparkling energy twirling into a tiny dance in the center of my body.

Gusto sat back and smiled, taking in the moment. Then he continued, saying, "Your spark has been fading, so small you could barely feel it. But it's never too late. Never, my friend. And hope is never, ever lost. You made a decision, and so here we are."

He patted my knee. "All it takes is a single moment of the kind of hope that says maybe-just-maybe and the kind of trust that says okay-yes, I-don't-understand-but-okay-yes. And the spark starts becoming a flame again. Just a single moment."

Everything Gusto was saying resonated with me. I wanted to hear more. As much as he would tell me. I said, "Before coming here, I kept getting a glimpse of something more, something bigger than that suffocating space I was in—I felt like I couldn't breathe—but then that 'something more' would disappear so quickly. I felt like I was between two worlds but living in neither. Or maybe I was in one, just not really living. Just going through the motions, over and over."

Gusto smiled. "When we started off on our walk today, there was one moment when you took a step, and you had one foot still on the beach and the other just off the ground, about to step into the jungle. See it?"

"Yes." I nodded, picturing that moment.

"That's where you've been. You have one foot cemented in parts of your life that aren't making you happy, and the other foot trying to pull you forward. The turmoil you feel? It's from saying no, not yet to that forward movement over and over."

Gusto tapped his chin with his finger. "Hmm... you need something. Yes. Somewhere to go when you feel so stuck. What do you need... I'm not sure... Anyway, you have one foot here and one foot begging you to go there. So you don't quite fit in anywhere in your life right now. No matter of it. It's okay. I think it bothers you, though. Yes?"

His words hit home. "It does. I'm starting to feel like I don't fit anywhere. I think I might've taken the wrong path somewhere along the way. I've... I made a lot of wrong turns." I wiped the tears and took a deep breath. "A *lot* of wrong turns. I think I'm expecting too much, that I should be able to be happy no matter what. Maybe I just don't know how to be happy. I think maybe I need to change—that I'm the problem."

"No, Ophelia. Just the opposite! The only thing you need to change is thinking you need to change. *Hold on to who you are.*

"Wrong turns? Maybe. Maybe not. Let's say yes, though. So you put on a pair of shoes that's way too tight and makes you walk funny and hurts. Not a problem... unless you keep wearing those same shoes. When you stop forcing a shoe to fit, you find a pair that does.

"You see, my Ophelia, the problem is," he held my gaze to make sure I was understanding, "you have forgotten who you are. I wouldn't change anything about you. Not a single thing. And there's something I've noticed: the more you're yourself, the more interesting your life is, the further your energy goes, the brighter your star is, the clearer your voice is, the more beautiful the world is. So ... embrace all of who you are, including your mistakes and challenges and imperfections and quirks. You're breathtakingly beautiful. In every way."

He shook his head. "Don't forget who you are, my Ophelia. Embrace it. Hold on tightly to it. Maybe that's where your understanding ends. Right there. But that's the matter of it all."

"I don't know how to remember. I have no idea who I am anymore."

"It's not so complicated. Just be 100 percent, I-trust-you-completely honest with yourself. And you'll see. The blinders will come off. The veils—which, by the way, you could always see through anyway—they'll come down. You'll suddenly see possibilities where there seemed to be none. Ophelia... it will set you free."

He gave me that knowing smile. "You're exactly where you need to be. Right now and always. You have many purposes and paths that are just for you. I know. Yes, I know. You think it's all been lost. Or it's too late. Or it never was to begin with. No. Remember ... life is beautiful. *Your* life is beautiful.

"For the moment, have fun. You know why? I'll tell you. Because it's good to have fun and not so good to go too long without it. Do something that's fun. Find fun. Know it again."

I liked that idea. It made me feel lighter. I wanted him to say it to me a million times. "Have fun?"

"Have fun!"

I smiled. "Okay. I'll have fun."

"Really? You will?"

I felt a hint of excitement. "Yes, I promise."

"Do you remember how?"

"Gusto!"

"A little teasing. But I do wonder," he looked at the top of my head, "how can you have fun if you're still wearing the sad hat?"

He stood up and walked over to an orange and pink hibiscus that was more delicate and exotic than any I had ever seen. Then he came back and handed me the flower. "The unhappy hat doesn't work for you anymore. It's time to add some color to your life. Have fun. Remember the matter of it."

I tucked the flower into the hat.

"Much better!" He smiled and said it was time for him to go, that the waves were calling to him. After he waved goodbye, I watched Gusto dance his way through our jungle path, stepping from side to side, hopping over crawling vines and ducking under branches.

When he was almost out of sight, he turned around, cupped his hands around his mouth, and shouted, "Yes! I know what you need!"

I couldn't wait to find out. But first, I went over to a banana plant taller than me and pulled one of the huge leaves that was barely hanging on. It came off easily, like it was time to. I took the small black pen I always carried with me out of my pocket, but when I tried to write on the banana leaf, it didn't work. The ink wouldn't catch, almost as if the leaf was saying, *No, not here.* I looked around for something else I might be able to write on. It felt important to write a reminder to myself about what Gusto had said. It was still so fresh in my mind. *The beach… the jungle… one foot here and one there…*

I ran back to the beach to where I had kicked off my flip-flops when we first started on our walk. The thick, white soles were perfect. Turning one flip-flop on its side, I quickly wrote the words I had been repeating in my head since Gusto left.

Don't give up. Instead, ask to be shown the way when I need help. With anything.

Who I am is a decision I make, and I can change mood hats whenever I want to. When in doubt, have fun… and then decide.

5. The Making of Statements

I became a photographer by default, the way a bird spreads its wings because that's what it's shown how to do. My husband had already built a reputation as a young, cutting-edge photographer before he met me, when I was lacking direction and not sure I wanted any. He assured me I could learn how to see the world through a lens, sometimes pulling it up close, sometimes holding it as far as my arms would allow. He said he would teach me. He needed an assistant anyway, so it became our excuse to be together. This was two weeks after he first met me, one week after he said, "You and I, we'll still be holding hands decades from now." I laughed at it all, at the idea of spending my life with someone who was so sure about us only a week after meeting, at the idea of entering a profession I knew nothing about. And yet, in that moment, I felt the gentle but sure hand of destiny at work. I felt like the luckiest person I had ever known.

He saw our future before I did, but together we created it. Within a year, we got married, and eventually I became comfortable behind the camera. My husband taught me how to look at a broken fence and see it as the ideal background to showcase the depth of beauty in the person sitting on it. He taught me to see the lives lived around the raw, splintered wood of the fence, most of the paint worn away. He taught me to see violet in a sunset where I had only found oranges and yellows. Soon, we were partners. Together we knelt on the ground, pulled a blooming orchid toward us, stood and smelled orange blossoms, deeply inhaling, and we talked about how to capture those aromas through a lens that had no capacity to capture such a thing. Together, learning from each other, we discovered new ways of bringing the confidence out of a shy teenager, how to wait long enough to capture the authentic laugh of an ninety-year-old, something even the successive clicks of a high-tech digital camera couldn't make up for if the timing was off.

We added a child to the picture. With the birth of our daughter, we created a family. Some women long to be a mother; it's an instinct that kicks in at a young age, before they can even define it. They simply know it's part of their destiny. I didn't know it until my daughter was born. From the moment I held her in my arms, I wanted nothing more than to love her better than I had ever loved anyone in my life. Lying there in the hospital, as she was breathing in the life she had just begun living, my world became so simple, so pure. I looked around the room, sparsely furnished, my husband on the chair next to the bed, our daughter in my arms, my husband's hand over mine, my hand cradling our daughter's, and I realized that in a matter of minutes, I had gone from caring deeply about a list of twenty, thirty, forty things to caring about three. Only three. Those three hands intertwined.

I don't know why we hurt the ones we love the most. I've tried to come up with an answer for that, asking again and again, Why do we do it? Why do *I* do it? But there isn't an answer that feels true; they all feel tinged with a hint of justification. And so I've decided it should simply be a statement: we often hurt the ones we love the most.

6. What Can't Be Ignored

I'd always wanted to body surf, so I decided it was time. At first, I trudged through the water, rushing out to get to the next wave, feeling the resistance against my legs as the water and I moved in opposite directions. *Let it come to you!*—I could practically hear Gusto whispering in my ear though he was nowhere to be seen. I eventually gave myself over to the timing and rhythm of the waves. If I caught one wave every ten minutes, that was fine. And if only one out of ten waves carried me all the way onto the beach, that was fine too. I floated. I somersaulted. I dove. I lay back. I let go. I let go of needing anything—of needing the experience to unfold according to any agenda.

What struck me most was that it brought a feeling I didn't expect: *freedom*—not just when I caught and rode a wave, but in the moments of stillness between. I realized that fun takes the heaviness away and puts things in perspective the way nothing else can. The entire time

I was in the water, all that mattered was the present moment; everything else seemed to slip away into the water that lifted me, buoyed me, and carried me.

It had been a long time since I'd believed in fun and made it a priority. I decided to do something about that.

* * *

Hours later, after a hike into the jungle, I returned to the beach, sat down, and dug my feet into the sand. I loved how the moist cold of the deep sand wrapped itself around my feet while the sun bathed the rest of my body in its warmth. I was more than content to just sit there waiting for Gusto, thinking about how fun existed when I simply allowed it to. I wanted more of it. It felt so healthy, so right—so good. So important, as Gusto had said.

I leaned back on my elbows and closed my eyes, deciding to give myself over to the present moment and all of its possibilities. As much as I tried to relax though, I kept getting distracted by a stinging sensation all over my body. When I was coming out of the jungle earlier, I had brushed against a prickly pear cactus, so I opened my eyes to see if some of the hair-like thorns were still stuck in my skin. I held my arms up at an angle I'd be able to see the thorns, but there were none. As I closed my eyes again, I realized the prickly feeling was worsening and the sun was beating down heavily on me, growing stronger and strangely more intense.

I opened my eyes again and looked back toward the jungle. It made sense, I knew, to go back and find shade... but I didn't want to. As the heat became visible, a mirage directly in front of me, I had an overwhelming urge to look directly at the sun, but I squeezed my eyes shut instead. Every bead of sweat stung, as if those toxic thorns I couldn't see were pushing their way out of my skin of their own accord. I tried to dig my feet deeper into the sand to find more coolness but gave that effort up quickly. Something about it didn't feel right. As nervous as I was with the direction I was taking, all I wanted to do was let myself sink into the heat. Further. Then further. Deeper into it than I thought I was capable of—until my breath slowed, calmed, and slipped into a steady rhythm...

Sometime later, I sensed it. Gusto was looking at me. I could feel his eyes on me, a slight reprieve from the heat. A breeze twirled around me as the sun ducked behind a canvas of clouds, and the heat disappeared as quickly as it had come, taking the prickling sensations with it. I opened my eyes and turned to Gusto.

He was sitting next to me with a pyramid of freshly picked mangos in his lap. He cut into one, sliced off a piece, and then ate it. "Have you been able to have thoughts about *anything* besides the mango? I haven't! Not at all." He sliced off a wedge and handed it to me.

I took the piece of mango and said, "What just happened?"

He looked at me in a way that suggested confusion, but part of me knew better. "Didn't you have fun?" he said.

"Just now?"

"No! Since we last saw each other!"

"Oh yes…" I took a bite of the mango, relishing its sweetness.

"Yes. So you were telling the poison that it wasn't welcome anymore," he explained as he cut more mango and handed the pieces to me. Then he gave me a coconut husk filled with milk-colored water and continued, "Poisonous thoughts like 'Life isn't fun' or 'Ophelia isn't fun' or 'Ophelia doesn't know how to be happy.' You don't need those. Poison isn't good for you. So you let those thoughts go. You chose heat and decided to sweat them out. An age-old trick. Works every time.

"But I will tell you. You didn't *have* to let go of them that way. You could have pictured the thoughts as floating bubbles and—just like that!—popped them. You could have decided not to think those thoughts anymore, sent them away on paper airplanes, and brought in new ones to hold hands with. But you wanted a physical sign that you had released them. You wanted to verify it—to make it true. You wanted an *experience*. Always choices, Ophelia."

"Well, it was definitely an experience," I said. "I feel like I've released something heavy and old—and somewhat toxic. Maybe I did need the heat. I feel clearer, like the space inside me is purified of something that was there before and isn't now."

I finished the drink and handed the coconut husk back to Gusto. He took it back without a word and continued carving pieces from one mango after another, stopping now and then to look up and breathe in the open expanse of sky above us. Then he looked at me and smiled.

I smiled back at him, stood up, did a little twirl, and sat back down next to him. "Do you like it?" I asked. I knew he had to have noticed my hair when he first saw me but that mangos always came before "too much talk." It was a work of art, even by my standards. After body surfing and then hiking, I had slumped onto the ground in the shade of the jungle. I absentmindedly started twisting my hair in my fingers... and hours later, the time had passed without me noticing. I had woven lemongrass into thick braids, found twigs to secure flower petals into wild, little twisted buns all over my head, pulled one strand of hair through another, always adding whatever treasure my eyes next came upon in the jungle. After that, I went to the beach to meet Gusto and, I realized now, to let go of the thought that life wasn't fun.

"I love it," he said. "You found fun."

"I really did."

"It's a must, Ophelia. It's so easy to forget that, to think other things are more important. They become number one, number two... and pretty soon, to have fun feels like a right you don't have. Something for when you have time. Something for when your responsibilities are… well, when will there ever be none? No. Have fun being you. Consider your life a scavenger hunt for fun. Why? Because fun is an elixir. Like mangos for me. It feeds you. It fixes. It heals.

"So then. How do you feel about having more fun in your life? Every day. Not to let a day for the rest of your life go by without remembering the matter of fun. To make it number one, two, three—nothing lower on any list."

I nodded and said, "I'm ready." I started listing off the reasons I was ready, one by one. The words tripped over themselves as they ran from my mind and tumbled over my tongue; I found myself having a lot to say and feeling the need to say it quickly.

When I finished my long list of reasons proving I was ready to make fun a priority, Gusto said, "Hmm. You sound almost convincing, but you talk so fast, it makes me wonder. Go inside, my Ophelia. Answer with your heart, not your head… I'll ask you in another way. Are you ready to change things?"

I wanted the answer to be yes. I *really* wanted it to be yes. But when I let myself feel the answer, I knew it wasn't.

"I wish I was," I said. "But deep down, for some reason, I don't think I'm completely ready." Then I admitted something I had recently begun to believe. "I think I have a *need* to be unhappy because I don't know how else to be."

Gusto stared at me for a moment and then burst into such an uproar of laughter that tears soon rolled down his cheeks. I couldn't help but notice how he took his time with his laughter, and soon I found myself laughing with him. Though I didn't know why I was laughing, I was aware of what a release it was.

When our laughter subsided, Gusto turned to me and said, "No, you're nothing of the sort. Apples and oranges." He jumped up, reached for my hand, and said, "Follow me. I want to show you something."

He led me into the jungle, winding his way between sprawling, white-striped spider plants. Finally we came to a tree that reached above the others, stretching its branches to touch the sky. A makeshift bamboo ladder with nearly forty rungs was leaning against the trunk.

I looked at Gusto and smiled. "You've been busy."

He started climbing. I followed him, step by step up the ladder. I didn't look down, and I didn't look up. Instead, I focused on all the insects lounging on the bark of the tree trunk watching Gusto and me pass by. When I finally reached the last rung at the top of the ladder where the tree forked into an opening, Gusto leaned down and helped me up onto a brilliant mess of branches that spread out, supporting a small bamboo platform. It was just big enough for the two of us to sit comfortably—more of Gusto's handiwork. I sat down next to him and looked around. We were above the roof of the jungle, and beyond the edges of the island, I could see the limitlessness ocean in every direction. A carpet of greens from the interlocking treetops surrounded us, so thick I wondered if I could walk across it.

"Did you do all of this for me?"

"Which came first? The chicken or the egg? I couldn't say, my friend. But what I do know is that this is a good place for you to be. Closer to the sky. You need to spend more time here."

"A tree house? That's what I needed?" I liked the idea.

"Yes, to pull you out of the mud when you're stuck in it."

Sitting cross-legged with my hands planted firmly next to me, I tilted my head back until all I could see was the cloudless sky above me. I realized then that it wasn't just above me, it was in front of me and behind me and even below me. I was a part of the airy expanse, and the weightless, drifting feeling that came with that understanding made me feel a little dizzy. I sat straight up and pushed my knees down, trying to connect with the platform I was sitting on—anything solid, anything connected somehow to the ground. As much as I loved feeling like I had stepped into a fantasy world above the treetops, I didn't think it was a place I could stay too long. I didn't have to say it. Gusto knew.

"What? Why not, my Ophelia? Wait… I know. I know!" He started laughing. "If your head is in the clouds, you can't think right! Well, maybe that's not so bad. Many people say to think before you act. Yes?"

"Yes."

"But not Gusto."

I laughed. "Not a surprise."

"I say *feel* before you act—before you speak, before you do anything. Feel first." He pointed to his belly and said, "Here. Right here. This is where you feel it."

I felt it. There was a pit in my stomach.

"What do you want, Ophelia? When you let yourself, what do you hope for? Where has that other foot been trying to take you? Feel and answer… without thinking so hard."

Not letting myself hesitate, I said, "I want to learn again. I want to grow something. I want to take old, worn-out things that seem to have no use and turn them into something beautiful. Like old, rusted pieces of metal—sculpt and weld them into something useful that I love looking at. Or a room. Take everything out, rip up the floors and strip all the walls until it's raw and empty. Then create a new space, being able to step back at any moment and love what I'm looking at, no matter where it is in the process of being built."

"I love it! Let's do it."

"But do I have to break something first? That's what I keep thinking. *Break it*—I hear it over and over in my head and…" Sadness and guilt surged through me, pictures quickly flashing one after another in my mind. "I've heard it for a long time. And then all I can see in my mind's eye is all this destruction. Is that you talking to me? Do things need to break before they can be fixed or turned into something better?"

"No, I'm not in your head; I'm in your heart. So I will tell you, it can be a beautiful gift to let things break or to even break them yourself. But if you think you always need to use a hammer and slam down very hard to do it, wait… it might not be time, and it might not be the way. And if only one room needs fixing, you don't need to break the whole house. Slow down. Always. Feel what's in your heart first. Then you'll know. Even now. What do you feel in your heart?"

"I feel like I'm just playing musical chairs with my life. I move from one chair to the next, around and around in the circle, but they all kind of look and feel the same. I never move out of the circle; nothing ever really changes. The game is something inside me—I know that. But I don't know how to stop playing it. I try to outsmart the game, but it's me I'm trying to outsmart, and I end up just moving faster from chair to chair."

Gusto looked pleased. "Yes," he said. "You want things to change—I understand. And they will. But first, slow down. You can't escape what's yours to be a part of until you've drunk the last juice of it. And you can't drink the juice of a mango until you've peeled the skin back and exposed the fruit."

"I don't understand. What does that have to do with musical chairs?"

"Nothing! And everything. I think in mangos. You think in chairs. So then, something inside you needs your attention. Yes. And if you try so hard to quickly force your way around from chair to chair, you only get dizzy. What you're trying to escape will follow you."

He smiled, patted my knee, and said, "Maybe no more moving from chair to chair. Stand in the center of the circle instead. Stand tall! Let yourself feel whatever it is you feel. I'll tell you why: because your feelings will speak to you. They'll show you what needs your attention. And when you give your attention to what needs it, you'll see an opening between the chairs. You'll know your way out. You'll be able to name the real game being played inside you. Then you'll remember you don't have to play that game anymore, or you can change the rules, and you'll find yourself ready—honestly ready—to have fun being you. To live a life that knows fun better than it knows anything else except love. Can you see it?"

"I can, but…"

Gusto put his finger to his lips and said, "Shhh… go inside yourself. You want to make changes to fall in love with yourself and your life again. Yes. But something is stopping you. You know what it is." He pointed to my heart and said, "Listen …"

As I sat on that platform that was our tree house, I looked around and let all my thoughts go, focusing only on the feeling of being in the center of the jungle's roof.

All the green surrounding me, the color, a vivid green light. It felt like a surreal permission to feel whatever I was feeling. I wasn't confident enough to stand tall in that high-up space, but I managed to sit still in it. To breathe. To relax. To allow my feelings to surface, as if rising from the ground below, starting deep in the roots, up through the thickness of the tree trunk, through the bamboo I was sitting on, into me, until what I was feeling had a voice in my heart I could hear. Soon enough, I realized I did know what it was, what was stopping me. And as absurd as it sounded to me, I let the words come out.

"Deep down… I don't actually want things to get better yet."

As soon as I said it out loud, the circle of chairs I had been picturing moved outward a few feet, expanding the circle, opening up a little space, making it easier to move around. The moment felt more manageable. I was still inside the circle but didn't feel so confused and closed in. More than anything, I felt less afraid. I had said it out loud. I admitted what I was most afraid of admitting, and in doing so, the fear lost some of its power.

From the way Gusto looked at me, I knew he was proud of me, like a parent whose child has just taken her first step. A little unsteady, a little unsure. But I did it. "Yes, Ophelia. Do you know how deliriously in love with honesty I am? No matter what it is—no matter what—if it's your truth, it won't destroy you. No, my Ophelia, it's the opposite. Honesty brings you back to life.

"So then, it's time to discover why you don't want things to get better yet. Yes. That feels better!" He stood up and smiled. "Observe. Notice. Then you'll understand what you just told me. Honesty will always tell you what you need to know. Be honest in your thoughts, and be honest about how you feel. With yourself and with everyone else. It's who you are, Ophelia. And until you come from that place of honesty, you can't fully move out of the circle of chairs you've been hopping between."

Reaching a hand out to help me up, he said, "So maybe it's not so bad to have your head in the clouds sometimes. Yes?"

"It's different. That's for sure. Something about it makes me willing to say and feel things I normally wouldn't let myself." I smiled. "Thank you for that, Gusto. And for this tree house."

"It's always my pleasure!"

He led me off the bamboo platform and down the ladder. As we walked back through the jungle to the beach, Gusto hunted mangos. I simply let myself feel the emotions circling through me, no matter what they were. When we reached the beach, before saying goodbye, he whispered, "Notice what you least expect to see." Then, with a wink, he was gone, leaving me to feel the spark inside me slowly coming back to life.

I pulled off my flip-flop, took the pen from my pocket and, using the smallest handwriting I could, wrote a reminder to myself.

I'm fun, and life is fun.
If any thought I have suggests otherwise,
I'm going to let it go. I don't need it.

When I'm stuck, I can be my own ladder.
Honesty—first with myself, and then with other people—
brings me out of even the deepest of ruts and back to life.

7. The Creation of Questions

It was day three of photo editing after the wedding in Bali. Everything had been unpacked, the suitcases put away. There was no more grocery shopping to be done. I had dropped off and picked up the dry cleaning. I had replaced a cracked faceplate on a light switch that had been bothering me for months. I even made a special trip out just to buy more liquid hand soap because the dispenser in the kitchen was only halfway full. We would need to add more. Eventually.

As I was standing in the kitchen trying to decide what to do next, what other errand I could run, the phone rang. It was our daughter. She said she would be coming home next weekend. No, nothing was wrong, she assured me. Her first semester in college was still going well, but... she had planned to... I have no idea what else she said.

I saw my husband walk out of our office toward the kitchen where I was standing. The slowness of his walk, that's all it took. I didn't need to see the look on his face. I didn't need to hear what he was about to say. I could feel it. He knew.

"What have you done?" he asked. So calmly. The sadness palpable.

That's when the unraveling began.

I don't know when the first thread was pulled. At some point, he and I had stopped asking the kinds of questions we often discussed when setting up for a photo shoot, taking pictures, or going through photos already taken. They were questions we used to talk about over coffee in the morning, driving to or from somewhere, getting ready—for anything—together, dining together, taking leisurely walks, drinking wine under a starry sky. During those times, we weren't talking about the photographs we were capturing and creating for other people; we were talking about our life. *What do you think of this setting? Do you like the background? Does something need to be moved around? Should something else be in the center of the picture? How might it look if I shifted positions? Or if you did? Is the light good? Can we see clearly? Where's the color? Do you see what I see? What are you looking at right now? What's your vision for how this should look? Does this person belong in the picture? Why is that person so far off in the background? Does this need to be cropped? Should we change how we're looking at this? Do we need to step back and see this from farther away? Are you satisfied with this? Do you love it? What can we learn from where this one went wrong? How can we add more color? How can we brighten this?*

Every so often, we'd take inventory of our camera equipment. As we grew in our profession, our needs changed. We were ready for more sophisticated lenses, more advanced tripods to steady the camera on rougher terrain, a camera that better lent itself to what we were trying to create. But we stopped asking questions about our day-to-day life. *Do you still have the basic things you need? Have your needs changed?*

We lost focus. We took more and more pictures of other people's lives and stopped deliberately creating and talking about our own. I can't say when the first thread fell loose—or the next or the next. It happens the same way old photos fade, the colors moving from vivid hues and bright contrasts and clear lines to sepia and gray tones and blurred distinctions, the substance decaying and the edges eventually tearing. How my husband and I once were, how we were as a family, how he once was, how I once was—like ancient photos, it all became so delicate, so fragile. Barely there, just traces left.

I didn't want to take those old photos and revive them. We had tried that, and it all still felt fixed. Repaired but still in the process of decaying.

Looking back, I know now that I wanted to create a new set of pictures. What I sometimes still wonder about is whether it was necessary to destroy the entire album to do that.

8. First Things First

Gusto was right. It was the last thing I expected to notice when I became willing to see whatever I saw. I couldn't wait to tell Gusto about it, but he wasn't at our usual spot on the beach when I went to find him. He had left a note for me, blackberries placed on a big fan palm, spelling out: *Come find me!*

Hide and seek, I realized. Gusto loved games. I headed straight for the jungle and spent the next hour sneaking around trying to find him. I looked in and around the cluster of mango trees, pretending the mangos were my spies and asking them to point me in the right direction. I headed up the ladder to the bamboo platform, talking to a parade of ants along the way, my cohorts in a secret mission. But he wasn't there either. I searched in every one of Gusto's favorite spots, even the ones he didn't know I knew about, jumping out each time, sure he would be there. But he never was. And after a while, I wasn't talking to mangos or bugs anymore. I was starting to talk to myself. I headed back toward the beach.

It was then, as I came out of the jungle onto the open beach, that I saw Gusto, straight ahead of me—jumping up and down, waving to me from the ocean. Right at that moment, a wave came, knocked Gusto down, and carried him, tumbling and still waving, halfway up the beach.

Dripping wet, he ran up to me and threw his arms around me, getting me just about as soaked as he was. "You found me! What took you so long?"

"I went into the jungle," I said.

"Well, I know that! I saw you!"

I realized Gusto had been there, right in front of me, from the moment I went looking for him. I hadn't even looked up to see him—I had simply turned and headed straight for the jungle.

"Sometimes what you're looking for is already there! Ta-da! Anyway, are you hungry?"

"No… well, yes… but I want to tell you what happened."

"First things first. My Ophelia needs food for the soul." He pointed to the fan palm. "Did you see this?"

"Yes, that's how I knew to look for you."

"Yes. Maybe. Or maybe…" He scooped up the black-berries and gave me a handful. Then he pulled back the palm and pointed to a small bunch of bananas sitting in a hole in the sand. "Ah-ha!" he said to the bananas. "I found you!" He lifted them out, slowly and carefully, as if they were precious cargo.

His excitement was contagious. We sat down and put our feet in the hole. After finishing the blackberries, Gusto tore off a small banana, handed it to me, and then began peeling one for himself.

"So then," he said, "this is good. Tell me what happened. You were looking to see what you least expected. Yes?"

"Right. The jungle seemed to be a good place to start. At first I started looking for signs, something unusual. After a while of seeing nothing strange or out of place, I decided to take a break from trying to see whatever it was. That's when I looked down and saw a *huge* snake slither out from the bush I was standing next to." Just the thought of how I felt in that moment made my stomach turn. "I've been terrified of snakes my whole life."

He laughed. "I know. Believe me."

"So, not sure whether to run away or stand completely still—how best to avoid panic and prevent the snake from striking out—I slowly stepped backwards, keeping my focus on it. We made eye contact, and it pulled me under its spell. Just like that. I've never felt anything like it. The snake took me into the rhythm of its life stages, and it was as if I was experiencing the word for the first time… *shed*… well maybe not the first time, but pronounced differently. The shedding of skin; I knew that's what the snake was showing me. As I imagined trying to shed a layer of me—letting go of any part of me—the idea felt more threatening than the snake's venom would have been. *You are not me.* I heard it spoken in the snake's language, four times, the emphasis on a different word each time. '*You* are not me,' the snake said. 'You *are* not me. You are *not* me. You are not *me.*' That's when the snake let go of its hold on me and pulled back into the bush."

"Ah, yes," Gusto said. "A soulful snake. So generous."

"That was just the beginning. My thoughts turned a quick corner after that, and I considered all the people in my life. All I could think was that I didn't want any of them to change either. I love them—exactly as they are. With their quirks and faults… there's a perfect beauty to each of them. I know that sounds strange, but that's what I felt… that I just really love them."

"Yes, yes, my Ophelia. Go on."

"It was a strange feeling, a really good feeling. And it felt so new, it stopped me. I just sat down—a ways from the bush, because I'm still not crazy about snakes—and took it in. Then, one by one, all the other things that make me happy found their way into my thoughts. I couldn't believe there were so many. And what I realized was that as much as I want some of the things in my life to be better or different, I still find happiness in so much just as it is."

"Yes," he said. "Yes, yes, yes. So you understand now why you haven't wanted things to get more colorful yet."

"Well, no… I'm still not sure why. Because I do want things to get… more colorful." There it was again. The pit in my stomach. "But the truth is, not all of me wants that."

Gusto looked at me and said, "Okay then. You need to move."

"What?"

"Yes, move. Move! Tango, run, climb—whatever your spirit calls for. Me? I'm going to have just one more of these bananas that are so happy I found them. Then I'm going to take a nap. You—move until it's time to rest. Then come back here. Rest. Be quiet and listen. You'll hear it. Just one word, Ophelia."

He looked at me as if waiting for me to say something and then said, "What are you waiting for? Go!" He started laughing and lay back in the sand, enjoying the last banana.

* * *

I decided the best way to move was to take a walk along the beach, but shortly into it, my legs had a will of their own, a momentum stronger than my original intention. I started jogging and soon after was running. I loved how the sand pulled at my feet each time they touched, making it harder and harder to maintain speed and impossible to keep any sort of fluid motion. I knew I looked awkward, pushing hard against the sand, propelling myself forward as fast as I could go. I kept thinking I was going to fall, but I didn't want to stop. It felt good to move, and though I wondered whether I was running back to something or forward to something, it didn't really matter. I liked that my legs ached, that my arms were tingling, and that I could feel my heart beating. A surge of adrenaline kept pushing me forward.

I reached the end of the beach, where the tip of the jungle curved around, and nearly fell to the ground, I was so tired. I stopped for a long moment to catch my breath and then headed down to the water and dove in. I swam one slow stroke at a time, sometimes carried by the current, at times fighting it. When I was finally done, I dragged myself out of the water and made my way down the beach to where Gusto was sound asleep, snoring softly.

As soon as I lay down, I felt the sand pulling me down into it. My body felt heavy with the pulsing of every muscle. I just let my body be, allowing it to let go, to rest. As exhausted and worn down as I felt physically, there was some intangible part of me that felt brand-new and energized. It was inside of me but not connected to any physical part of me. I could see through it as I pictured it. Sparkling light. I moved into that space of clarity that was anything but empty. And it was then that I heard the voice Gusto had promised me I would. A crystalline voice from deep inside me.

Just as he had predicted, it said only one word.

I embraced the single word for a long time, holding it, peering into it, feeling it. Becoming it. Allowing myself to be embraced and absorbed by it. Then, when I sat up and opened my eyes, Gusto was sitting beside me, smiling as always. I knew he would remain silent as we sat for a little while, looking out across the endless slate of deep blue glass. Then, as bands of orange and pink gently brushed across the sky and the sun slowly hid itself behind the horizon, I looked at Gusto and invited him in.

"So then, my Ophelia, what was the word?"

"Gratitude." I inhaled deeply and smiled. It was still there. "It smells like orange blossoms. I can feel it, too—waves of emotion ebbing and flowing, drowning out everything else. And I can see it—tiny sparks of light dancing in the air right in front of me and all around me. It's seeped into every one of my senses. That single word."

Gusto nodded. "Yes. Tell me more. Tell me what you're grateful for."

After telling him about all the things, big and small, that made me feel lucky and thankful and happy, I looked at him and realized I could go on forever. As I came to that realization, he traced a figure eight in the sand.

"You see, the only way to move forward, to let that foot take you where you want to go, is to take the time to be grateful for what's working *right now*. To see what is colorful already. To see the gifts in being exactly where you are—no matter where you are.

"If I eat something bitter and keep the taste in my mouth, I can't taste the juiciness of the next bite, even if it's something sweeter. If my taste buds are filled with resentment for that bitter fruit, there's just no space for me to taste anything different.

"My Ophelia, resentment and bitterness weigh so much. They're so heavy, like big suitcases filled with boulders. So, as you can imagine, they make it hard to move forward. Trudge. Trudge. Slow movement. Too much dragging with you. But! When you feel only gratitude, you're light. No suitcase, no baggage. So much easier to lift your foot and step forward.

"No matter what's happening inside or around you, there are *always* gifts. Gratitude has no limit; it stretches out forever in every direction. When you give gratitude all the names it goes by, its endlessness begins to unfold before you. Suddenly, you find yourself having more and more reasons to feel lucky. Interesting thing. Want to know why? Because, Ophelia, when you give attention to what's working, what you're grateful for, you see the gifts—in each moment and each day. The more you're willing to see them, the more they show up. If you believe you're the luckiest person in the world, you *become* the luckiest person in the world. When you believe you have so much to be grateful for, you *create* so much to be grateful for. You see it?"

"Yes." I could even taste it.

"So then, now that you remember gratitude, are you ready for things to get colorful and better?"

Before answering, I got quiet and still inside so I could feel the answer. No pit. No resistance. "Yes. I'm ready."

"Yes!" Gusto stood and said, "Goodbye for now, my friend. Let things get so much better. So much clearer. You know how. Yes?"

"I think so."

"No, Ophelia. *Know so.* Believe you're the luckiest person in the world. Expect it. Know it. Because you are. And the world is wildly lucky to have you in it. Very, very lucky."

I got up and hugged him. "Thank you—for being you."

Gusto bowed and, without saying a word, picked up the palm frond that had been covering the bananas' hiding place, wrapped it around his shoulders, and began walking away—a king draped in the oddest and finest of garments.

Before I lost sight of him, I took my pen and added to the notes on the side of my flip-flop.

I can change any part of my life I want to, whenever I want to. But I'm not going to try to change who I am. What I really want is to become more of who I am.

When I look closely at what makes me happy and what I'm grateful for, I can move on when it's time to— from anything—without any bitterness, fully able to taste the sweetness of what's next.

9. The Volume of Words

It had been two days since my husband came out of the office and said, "What have you done?" With each passing hour, we drifted further away from each other, and all I kept thinking was, *How do you bridge two sides when both are sinking?* On that Friday afternoon, as she had said she would, our daughter arrived home for the weekend. She came in the door having no idea what she was entering.

After strained hellos and a building tension, my husband led my daughter outside to the back patio. I stood in the kitchen, my hands resting heavily on the table for support, not even pretending to be busy. I watched them through the glass doors, hearing a static-filled, muffled conversation through the open kitchen window. My husband telling her about something in a quiet voice. I heard my name. *Mom.* Again and again. My daughter looked inside at me, then back to her father. Her face went from curious to confused to a sadness that shattered a part of my heart that had started beating the day she was born. I felt its pieces scatter inside me, piercing, pointing.

The two of them spent the majority of the evening in our home office, the door open—a gesture on my daughter's part, I had no doubt. Her sensitivity would necessitate that, her way of asking me not to shut myself out. It was an invitation I didn't want to accept. Finally, she left the office and went to bed. I looked at the clock. 7:42. Our eighteen-year-old daughter, usually so full of life, ready to stay up late talking or just being together or going out with her friends, went to bed at 7:42 on a Friday night. I felt myself breaking.

The words and emotions were swirling and building inside me, and I knew that if I didn't start letting them out, they would consume me. My husband was still in the office. He was on the phone—again. He had been making call after call all day and straight through into the evening.

"I tried to tell you," I said after he hung up.

"Not loudly enough, Ophelia. Not *nearly* loud enough." He picked up the phone to make another call.

They were the last words we spoke to each other for days.

10. The Voice that Beckons

When I found Gusto on the beach, he waved me over and patted the sand next to him, motioning for me to join him. He was taking little bites of what looked like the bright pink and green flowers that were budding from cactuses throughout the jungle.

"Are you eating a flower, Gusto? Where are the mangos?"

"No mangos today. Today, we're eating pitaya, the dragon fruit! Variety is spicy."

"You mean, variety is the spice of life?"

"No… I mean variety is spicy. It adds spice. It's flavorful. Yes?"

Gusto was in rare form. My favorite. I decided to have some of what he was having. Before I even asked, he took a pitaya from the pile next to him, split it open with his pocketknife, and handed it to me. He suggested I eat it however I wanted to, but to be sure to eat the little black seeds as well.

Gusto squeezed the halves of the pitaya and then drank the juices. "Nothing like it!" He reached for another pitaya and said, "So, my friend. How does it feel to be so lucky?"

"It feels really good. In fact, I feel a little guilty for wanting so much more, considering how lucky I already am."

"Ah, yes, you and your guilt. You know, you should maybe look through your closet and throw away more hats. Anyway, you often think that things aren't as bad as they could be, so you should just be happy with them. You have so much to be happy about, so who are you to want more? Yes?"

"That's what I've been wondering."

"No! No! I'll tell you a story. The weather was moody, and it made some fruits not so ripe yet. I searched and searched and finally found a rollinia tree filled with fruit ready to eat. I had never come across one before and was very excited because I knew the rollinia was supposed to taste like lemon meringue pie. Yes! Well, I peeled back the spines and sank my teeth into the fruit. Oh, it was sour! I winced and puckered my mouth. But, no matter of it. I would try again. I took another off the tree and this time cut it in half and tried squeezing the juice out first. Nope. My stomach hurt from the pain of it. I tried this with the fruit, and I tried that. Finally, there were no more ways to try it. All I knew then was that I didn't love the fruit.

"Now, I could have said, 'Well, I'm lucky to have any fruit, so I should just learn to be happy eating the rollinia.' Or I could have said, 'Yes, it leaves a bad taste in my mouth, but at least it's digestible.' But then Gusto would not be Gusto! No. Was I grateful for the sun and the sand and the jungle and many, many other things? Was I grateful for being Gusto? Of course! And for even the rollinia? Yes! But I heard a little voice calling to me. It was so quiet, whispering, 'Come find me, Gusto!' I said, 'I don't know where I'll find another fruit. But I don't want to eat this fruit anymore. I don't enjoy it enough. There must be something better.' And yes, my friend, shortly after, I was introduced to… Do I even need to tell you? The mango! It was the voice of the mango that had called to me! Do you see? You really should listen to me. Yes?"

I smiled. "Yes."

"Be grateful—oh, yes. But that doesn't mean stand still. It doesn't mean don't want more. You can move forward, on to more color and texture—being grateful each step of the way. If you want more, there's a reason for it! You're meant to be more, have more, do more! Remember when you were wearing the unhappy hat? Do you know why you were unhappy?"

"Tell me," I said.

"Because you felt a pull forward—to dreams and magic and life itself—to growth and movement. But you were standing still, and so nothing was moving or changing. Nothing was *becoming*.

"Listen to the voice that calls to you. There's only one of you, and you bring a taste to life no one else can. If you hear a voice saying, *Yoo-hoo!* there's a reason. Follow it… Follow your heart, my Ophelia. Trust that voice in your heart that urges you forward, that says, *Come. Follow me. I'll lead you.*"

He leaned in closer and spoke in a whisper, telling me a secret. "One thing you should know about the rollinia. It was more than okay without me. The matter of it is that when you let go of something that's really just not for you, it's better off without you. Whether it's a fruit, a place, a person, a hat, a job, a spice. Anything. You see, when I put the rollinia down and moved on, other people were free to enjoy it without the bitter, sour taste in my mouth eventually affecting their own pleasure. And the rollinia could be appreciated exactly as it was.

"Follow your heart—and then *keep* following it—and you will know happiness… the kind that doesn't disappear. The kind that grows."

Gusto stood up and exclaimed, "This is your life! Grab hold of it, shape it, and create it! Make it a life you're excited to live. Why not? There's no reason, Ophelia. No reason not to."

He smiled, crouched in front of me, and spoke softly. Another secret. "There's nothing stopping you. You'll see. When you decide to follow your heart, everything falls into place one piece at a time. Life starts to work. It flows. And you fall in love with it because you've fallen in love with yourself and all that you surround yourself with. There's no reason to do anything other than live a life you love. Do you see it?"

"Yes." I felt the truth of his words surge through me.

Gusto stood again and held his arms out wide. "Want as much as your heart wants. You're meant to. You know this. Are you ready?"

"Yes."

"You're smiling."

"I know." I smiled even more.

"I like seeing you smile. Okay then. To be grateful doesn't mean to be full of something that grates at you. It means to be thankful as you create a life that is full of everything great. Ha! Gusto is a poet!" He looked around like something suddenly caught his attention. "Do you hear that?"

I listened but didn't hear anything. "What is it?"

He looked around again and then whispered, "A voice, calling to me."

Ah-ha. Of course. "A mango?"

"No! This time it's a miniature pineapple! I don't know why! But I'll go find out." And with that, he was on his way, a detective searching for clues he was sure to find.

I, on the other hand, took out my pen and wrote down what I was sure I didn't want to forget.

Being grateful isn't about staying where I am
in order to prove to myself that I'm thankful
for parts or even all of it. It's about being thankful
as I fill my life with more greatness.

Listen to the voice that calls to me. Always.
Filled with courage and wild trust,
allow my heart to lead me.

11. The Volume of Silence

The next morning, Saturday, our daughter came out to the back patio. She sat down next to me, a stack of photographs in her hand. I had no doubt they were from the wedding in Bali.

"Are you okay, Mom?"

I looked at her. The words fell back down inside me.

She started leafing through the photos and then quietly said, "I just keep thinking, what if it was *me?* What if it was my wedding?" I couldn't pull my gaze from her—her face, her eyes staring at the photos. I didn't look down to see which ones she was looking at. "What happened?" she said. "And what about Dad? Do you realize what it's done to him? Have you *seen* him?"

I don't know any other time in my life when I was at such a loss for words.

When I didn't answer, she got up, leaving the photos on the chair beside mine.

A half hour later, I heard her drive off, and I knew it would be a long time until I saw her again. Children are like that. They can sense when the space of their home is no longer their own, when it belongs to two different people than the ones they left behind. They instinctively know when they need to go through a waiting period, to be birthed again into something new, someplace new, to two people who are once again ready for them.

I looked at the chair next to mine and picked up the stack of photos, not knowing what I would see, but knowing what I would not.

12. The Matters of Choosing and Creating

I sat on the beach and watched how the shore seemed to pull the waves in only to release them again. I thought about what I really wanted in all the different areas of my life, what I was being pulled toward. I wondered where my heart would lead me if I let it. The more I thought about it, the more surprised I was that I still didn't really know. As I hoped, after a while of sitting with so many unanswered questions and then wishing Gusto was there to help me understand, he showed up.

He sat down next to me and said, "So you think you don't know."

I smiled because I love how Gusto, when he chooses to, gets straight to the point. "No. I have no idea."

"I see. I'm not sure that's true."

It felt a little accusatory. And where were the mangos?

"I think you pretend you don't know what you want, because if you said what it was and really felt the maybe of it, you might have to stand up and do something about it. You would become responsible for the matter of it."

Where's this coming from? I thought. *Why is he being like this?* I didn't like where the conversation was going—or his tone. I decided to ask him straight out. "Are you saying I'm lazy? Or irresponsible?"

"Oh no. Only that as long as you decide you're undecided, you don't have to do anything. Days go by. Weeks. Then years. And still, you're where you're at."

I turned away from Gusto and stared out at the waves crashing in front of us. They had to have been at least twenty feet tall. Building, building, building—and then crashing. I felt like them. I liked the way they pounded the sand when they fell. For the first time since coming to the island, I felt myself shutting down and closing off from Gusto.

He sat next to me, uncharacteristically silent. I knew we were at a standoff and that I had a choice to make. Something about his stillness and calmness made that clear. I decided to ask myself, *What do you want in this moment?* The answer surfaced immediately: *clarity.* Just like when the waves were at their peak, right before they crashed. There was clarity in that moment—I could see into the water, see the fish riding the wave. I could see into the depths of the ocean. That's what I wanted. That kind of clarity. I turned to Gusto with a willingness to at least hear him out and gave a nod that promised nothing more.

"You're afraid because you believe that what you want isn't up to you," he said. "That it's the matter of someone or something other than Ophelia. So then it is. And when you decide that, you get disappointed. Of course. And then you decide to never again want anything. It's safer, you decide. But it's one of the most dangerous decisions you can make. Because when you want nothing, you care for nothing. You see, it begins with what you believe, and it ends up in what you see. You've decided to believe your life isn't up to you—because it's up to someone else or because you don't know what you want yet. Really, Ophelia? You can have and do and be anything you want. But you refuse to want because then you'll have to do and be."

I started feeling irritated but tried to be patient. "Gusto... there are *so* many parts of my life I have no control over."

"Not true, Ophelia. Of other people's lives, yes. Of the sky's weather, yes. But of you and your life? No. And your weather? No. It's no one else's fault. No one else's credit. No one else's responsibility."

"Gusto—"

"No. It's just not true at all. You can convince yourself but not me."

Not wanting the conversation to go any further, I stood up to leave and said, "I don't think you understand what my life is like when I'm not here on this island with you."

He shook his head. "You're not a victim."

"I never said I was!"

"That's not the matter of it. It's this: if you say there's a piece of your life you can't control, then you're shouting, 'I'm a victim.' And you're giving away responsibility. Walking into every door you've ever known, handing out a flyer that says, *Do you want my responsibility?* Then calling out, *Hey, you over there, do you? Or how about you? Come on! Just take it.*"

That did it. "You have no idea what you're talking about, Gusto. It's so easy for you, being the eternal optimist. Sometimes I think your head is stuck in the clouds. *Stuck,* Gusto. Making you ridiculously naïve. You're like a child. Happy this, happy that. Mangos that talk to you. How can you talk about responsibility? What are *you* responsible for?"

"The deepest happiness ever known."

I wanted to punch him. "Right. Well, when you live in paradise with nothing to care about but your 'deep happiness,' it's pretty damn easy to fulfill that responsibility."

"But that's the only thing *you're* responsible for, Ophelia. Your happiness. And by the way, I live with you, wherever you are. I just take the island with me."

"Are you kidding? Where have you been then? Did you bring your hammock with you? Have you been sleeping the last few years? And how about the last five months? *The only thing I'm responsible for is my happi-ness?* You have no idea what real life is like—the day-to-day of it. The sadness. The bad things that happen. *Just happen,* Gusto. And the bad things we do. That I do—yes, me. You have no idea about the disappointments or what it's like to disappoint yourself and everyone else. You have no idea what any of it is like. The absurdity. The mistakes. The hurt. The goodbyes. You have no idea what it's like to be at the mercy of circumstances and other people and my own shortcomings and flaws and—things that are very *real.* I don't care what you say. I *don't* have control over my life!"

And with that belief deeply felt and loudly asserted, I experienced one of the most terrifying feelings I'd ever felt. I was pulled out of my body back to previous moments in my life as an observer. I felt grounded in nothing, at the whim of all the events and people in those defining moments—like a tennis ball getting tossed around, volleyed high up here and then slammed down over there. I was the ball between hundreds of players and their racquets. I had no voice. I had no say.

I'm not sure how long that experience lasted, but it drained every bit of energy I had.

"Shhh," Gusto said before I could say a word when it was over.

"I can't—"

"Not now," he said. "Rest." I laid my head on his shoulder, and within seconds, I was sound asleep.

* * *

Gusto must have moved me after I fell asleep, because when I woke up I had a blanket of pale yellow leaves and a pillow made of sand. I looked at him waiting patiently and couldn't believe I had been so angry with him. I sat up and immediately felt nauseous, the dizzying feeling of being tossed around with no say still within me. I wanted to be done feeling that way, and I knew what that required of me, so I told Gusto I wanted to take control of my life. I wanted to accept responsibility for my happiness. I asked him to remind me how to do it.

"Okay," he said, nodding. "I think you're afraid. Because wherever there's anger, there's fear at the bottom of the pile."

It struck a chord. "I might be."

He put his arm around me and said, "What are you so afraid of?"

I looked down at my hands in my lap. It felt childish, but I said it: "Of not getting what I want."

"Yes. Not getting what you want. Hmm…" He stood up and began his version of pacing, random footprints in the sand. Here, there, then in a circle, until he stopped and said, "Yes! I think I know the problem. The word *get*. That's it! What if you took that word away—used *creating* instead. Try it so I can hear…"

"Okay… I'm afraid of not creating it. Of not creating what I want." It felt and sounded so different than *I'm afraid of not "getting" it.* When I used the word "create," it felt like it was all on me, all up to me. The word "get" felt like I was at the mercy of someone or something else. Just like that, the nausea slipped away, and I felt like I could breathe deeply again.

"So much better! I want to celebrate!" He looked like he was considering running off to find something to feast on but then thought better of it. "You have beliefs. Yes?"

"Yes."

"So, they're full of power. If you want to take control of your life, take control of what you decide to believe.

"When you shouted *I can't control my life!,* you really believed you had no power. You gave it gas with your anger and fear. You wanted very much to prove your Gusto wrong. So all you could feel or see or taste was being without any power. The bigger the beliefs and the emotions that hold hands with those beliefs, the bigger the experiences.

"You need to pull your power back, the power you have given away over time. Yes?"

"That feels right. Yes. For sure."

"So then. Your beliefs pave the road for how your life happens. If you believe in a bumpy, broken-up road with many detours and hazards, and that's what you think about and give your emotions to, then of course your life will be a very bumpy road with many things in the way. If you believe in a smooth road with gentle, winding curves—one that's perfectly paved and has no potholes—you already know what comes next. The ride will be as you truly believe it will be. Because, you see, even if you did hit what someone else might call a pothole, you wouldn't see it that way.

"Do you see the gift in this? What do you believe?"

"Honestly, Gusto, I don't think it matters because a belief can't make things so. It can't change reality."

He started laughing and sat down. "My Ophelia. You're so stubborn today. But that's good. You're being true. So then. What would happen if I didn't believe there was any fruit on this island?"

"There would still be fruit on the island," I said. "That's exactly my point."

"Yes. But would there be fruit on the island in *my reality?* Because, you see, if I really believed there was no fruit here, I wouldn't be able to see it even if it was sitting right in front of me. You could be sitting there eating a delicious mango, saying, 'Look, Gusto! It's fruit!' But if I didn't believe it was possible for fruit to be here, and I didn't expect to see it and didn't want to see it—because I had to be right!—then I wouldn't be able to see it. I would see it as something else and maybe even tell you that you're having delusions."

"But, Gusto, that just means you would be wrong. Reality is reality."

"Ah, yes. Reality is reality. Then, my friend, what if the reality is that anything is possible? That every belief is a bulldozer that carves each road you take… and you spend your whole life believing you're not the driver, that you're just along for the ride? Might that be just like me believing there's no fruit on this island?"

I saw his point but wasn't fully convinced.

"You know what your heart most wants—in every moment. Yes?" he said.

"When I decide to be conscious of it, I usually do, but I can't say I believe it's always up to me."

"But it is!"

"Okay, actually, I do kind of see that. Maybe it's that I don't believe what I want is always realistic."

"Then of course it will not be."

"But I can't kid myself, Gusto! I can't pretend I think things are possible when I don't really believe they are."

"Yes. And that's a very good thing. Because honesty begins with yourself."

"Then where does that leave me?"

"Where you're always left! With a choice! Take a moment. Right now. Imagine those metal scraps you were talking about. Finding each piece, gathering them, sorting them, working with them... How would it feel?"

I closed my eyes and started picturing it... and then soon found myself elsewhere. There was a large, rectangular scrap of red-rusted metal, curled at one end, in a neighbor's yard. I had never noticed it leaning against the fence. I saw myself asking if I could use it; they had no use for it, agreed right away. We ended up talking for the first time even though we had been neighbors for months. Later, walking. Early morning. Leaning down in the most unlikely of places and finding more treasures, different from what I had set out looking for. Mixing cement. Plugging in a hot-glue gun. Clearing a huge, old, wooden table—underneath it, hearts etched into it from the artist it used to belong to, his lover's name inside the heart. The warmth of copper. The sturdiness of pewter. Wooden poles, waiting to be sanded and varnished. My hands around them. Sawdust on the floor…

The shift in me was tangible. I opened my eyes, turned to Gusto, and said, "Exciting. That's how it feels—really exciting. My hands almost feel like they're touching it all right now."

"Yes. Now. Imagine a voice in your head saying to you: 'You can't do that. It's impossible. You won't find the scraps. You don't know how to use the tools. It's not for you to do.' Imagine believing that. How does that feel?"

It felt like mud. Heavy and dark, pulling me down. "Not good. And not right."

"Then do something about it."

"Like what?"

"Change it, my friend. Change your belief. This won't be the first belief you've changed, and it won't be the last. Beliefs are choices. You can change them."

The excitement inside me was building; I could feel it. "How?"

"Step out of your head and into your heart. Your head can throw one *no* after another at you, like darts popping a balloon—all the reasons why maybe you shouldn't believe that what you want is possible. Your head can easily confuse you. Your heart will not do that. Your heart sees clearly. Unlike your mind, it doesn't hold hands with only two things—what you've been taught and what you've experienced. That's all your mind knows, but your heart, it's not limited like that. Your heart holds hands with *all* possibilities, and so it will always tell you what's true.

"So you have a choice. Listen to your head or listen to your heart. It's always your decision. Interesting thing, my friend. You have no problem letting yourself believe that things could easily get darker or worse, but you have a hard time letting yourself believe things could easily get better or more colorful. One is not more difficult than the other. You choose."

He had a point there. "Do you believe that we're meant to live a life we're in love with?" I asked.

"Just look at me! Then you'll know not only what I believe, but also every thought I decide to let stay and every emotion I say yes to. My Ophelia, believe!

"Believe that what you want—whatever it is—it's all possible. You have it in you to create anything you want in your life. *You* do. Anything, Ophelia. You don't have to depend on anyone or anything else to 'get' it. Many people help you—yes. But if someone or something says, 'No, you cannot have what you want,' you just say what the matter of it is: It's not up to them! It's up to you!

You're in control of your life. And everyone else is in control of theirs."

I knew he was right. *It was up to me.* That's what I had been most afraid of, but something switched in me with Gusto's explanation. Believing that whatever I wanted was up to me made me feel empowered and excited.

Before going our separate ways to explore and experience the island independently, as had become part of our routine, I had one more question. "It was different this time, Gusto. No fruit, no feast, no adventure. Even you were different. Why?"

He just smiled. And with that smile, he sent my question back to me. That's when I understood and knew the answer: I created it. According to my beliefs, a serious discussion required a serious setting. I decided I might just do something about that belief. I missed the mangos.

There were so many words from our conversation I wanted to keep with me. So as Gusto went on his way, I took off my flip-flop and made some notes.

I have control over my life. I'm not a tennis ball.

I get to be responsible for my own happiness.

I don't have to worry about whether or not I'll get what I want because I can create what I want.

Every belief is a choice. I can change them,
let go of them, and create new ones.
It's simple; just step out of my head and into my heart.
Feel what's true for me.

13. The Weight of Thread

I sat on the patio late into the night. There were thousands of pictures of the relatives and friends who had flown to Bali for the wedding, from their arrival through to their departure. My husband had taken those photos. Airport hugs, silhouettes watching the sunset, glasses raised, arms held out in dance, children giggling, a father's soft glance, shoes kicking up petals.

The bride and groom were my responsibility. It was the first time my husband had given me that role. Normally, the couple was his singular focus. On the way to Bali, on the plane, I had asked him why he wanted to switch roles. "I don't know," he said. "It just feels right."

Instead of capturing one of the most important days of the bride and groom's life with smiles, eye contact, a hand on an arm, fingers caressing a leg, cascading hair, a head resting on another's shoulder, I had captured a withering tree branch, barely hanging on, off to the side from where the couple had posed, the struggling wings of a fly in the air inches from where their faces would have taken center stage in the photo, the rusted metal of the room number rather than the bride and groom looking at each other, standing in front of the door to their honeymoon suite. I had taken exactly 2,164 photos. None of the bride or groom. Not one. They were the ghosts, their presence felt but missing from every photo.

The bride and groom sued, as did the parents.

Word spread quickly. Cancelations piled up until there was almost nothing else to cancel—future shoots we had been locked in for. I could hear my husband on the phone in the office. Cordial, professional, taking the high road. "Yes... No, I understand... Okay, thank you. I appreciate it... You too." My husband didn't argue with their breach of contract.

Our business, my husband's reputation in his circle of peers, it was ruined in a matter of forty-eight hours. Thread after thread unraveled, one tug affecting another, causing the entire fabric of it all to loosen, to separate, and then to fall apart.

As hard as that was, nothing broke me like the single thread that held strong: my husband never told anyone except our daughter that I was the one responsible for the nonexistent pictures of the bride and groom.

14. The Question of How

It wasn't long before I went searching for Gusto. When I found him on the beach, he had mangos already peeled and ready to share. A feast again. I gladly accepted one and then wasted no time before telling him what was going on. I explained how I believed that anything I wanted to create in my life was possible—because I didn't have to depend on any one person or thing for it—but I didn't know what to *do* to make it happen… any of what my heart most wanted.

Gusto smiled and said, "No problem! Any time you don't know what to do, you know just what to do! Nothing. Give all of your attention to what you want and then stand in the center of your life while the *how* of it finds its way to you."

"But when you decided you didn't like the rollinia, didn't you go looking for a different kind of fruit to eat? You did something about it."

"Oh yes! I ran around like a crazy man. I ran in every direction but had no direction at all. All around the island. And that just made me a little dizzy and very tired. So I decided to rest. I found a tree to lean against. I sat and sat, leaning against the trunk until something told me to look up. Yes, my friend, I was leaning against the giant mango tree in the jungle. When I saw the hundreds of mangos above me, I laughed and laughed. You know why? Because I had passed that tree many times when I was running all around the island in a hungry frenzy."

Gusto leaned forward and drew a big circle in the sand, around and around. Then he took the pit from a mango he had eaten and placed it in the middle. "Sometimes what you need to do is just stand still and believe. Give your attention to what you want. Expect that it will happen. Feel it happening. Know that the answers will come and that when the time is right, you will know exactly what to do. My Ophelia, do you feel the relief in that?"

I couldn't hide my skepticism. He looked away and then looked at me again. Finally, with the tiniest hint of exasperation, he said: "Just be the pit!"

I picked up one of the pits and held it for a few minutes, aiming to connect with it—the still center in a burst of a life. It felt good. "I can do it."

"Good!" he said. "The answers will come! Plop. Plop. Every one of them. They always do. Always. Right now, if you don't know where to put your foot, all you're meant to do is stand tall with both feet where they already are and believe with the fullness of who you are. Believe in what you want!

"Soon you'll feel a pull toward doing something specific. Once the mango tree and I found each other, I eventually needed to climb it and pick the mangos. After not much time, I felt a pull to do it. Why? Well—as I soon found out—because they were ripe and ready! Don't take action just to take action. It's so tiring. Just thinking about it…" He took a deep breath and then exhaled loudly. "Much better. Anyway, forced action doesn't lead you where you want to go. Slow down, my Ophelia, and wait. You'll feel *moved* to do something particular. Very different from doing something just because it's a habit or you're not so patient or someone tells you to do it.

"When you feel a push inside you, even if it's just a hint of a push, follow it. A tiny thought, a little idea, a whisper. Maybe you're moved to walk down a certain street. Maybe talk to someone. You don't know why. It could be anything. Maybe it's something you're excited to do, maybe something that's not easy to do. No matter of it. And no matter what result you see or don't see because of it. Just do it. Step by step.

"Every time you lift your foot, it will land you some-where, and eventually you'll be closer to what you want. And the more you listen to those little pushes inside you, the louder they'll get. You'll see. When you listen, it's like those little pushes that are so wise inside you say, 'Finally! Ophelia is listening to herself! She's ready!' So then they'll push you here and then there, faster and more often. Follow them, follow them, follow them! Each one. Soon, you'll be off in a new moment. The answers will have come. Changes will have been made. Those pushes inside you will have taken you exactly where you want to go, and you'll have created exactly what you wanted to create in your life. And then! You'll be able to look way back and see how taking each tiny step that seemed to matter not at all ended up making all the difference.

"When something inside you says to do something, to take a step, do it. Just do it, Ophelia. That's part of the fun of being in control of your life.

"For now, until you hear a whisper or loud voice inside you telling you the next step, let the *how* of it find its way to you. I see so much beauty in that! Don't you?"

"I do…"

He smiled. "Ah-ha! I knew it! You're feeling a little push now, yes? A step to take!"

"I think so," I said, "but it doesn't make any sense to me."

"Oh! Those are the best kind! What is it telling you to do?"

"Let go. But what does that mean? Let go of what?"

"You tell me."

I said the first thing that came to me. "Everything. All of it. Everything except being here with you right now."

"Oh, this is so happy. I can hear it. The voice inside you is saying, 'Don't worry, relax, the universe has the metal to the pedal.' So then do it! Let go for this moment. You see, if I'm holding a mango, not cutting or peeling it, just holding it, it's connected to my hand, and I'm attached to it. Sometimes it helps to hold on, sometimes not. But gripping and squeezing? It pulls all the juice and life out. Always. You've been holding on tight to what was and how you think things are supposed to be. *Supposed to—* not my favorite words. It does no good to squeeze too hard. Detach and let go. Unclench your hand. Let go. Then allow."

The thought of letting go, dropping any question that started with "But how," and taking on the role of *allowing* instead of pushing and forcing—it caused an immediate shift in me. One by one, I let go of everything I had been holding so tightly to. It felt like the flip of a hundred switches within me.

"It feels good, yes?"

I smiled. "Yes."

"And standing still, my friend, when it's time to do so, feels very good too. Do you want to see?"

I told him I did.

Gusto looked at me and said, "Well, then…"

We stood up.

He lifted his arms and looked up to the sky, and then he stretched his arms wide open. With one deep breath after another, he looked all around—to the ocean, the jungle, the beach—focusing on each space, one at a time, taking it all in. Then he closed his eyes, stilled his breath and his body. I followed his lead and did the same.

My entire body relaxed as I slowed my breath, let go of all thoughts, and opened to only the movement that surrounded me. I could feel the ocean, the circling tides and the pushing and pulling of the waves. I could feel the air swirling, gently tumbling over and around itself. I sensed the individual grains of sand shifting, slowly, so slowly, one at a time, each affecting the next. I could feel the branches on the palm trees swaying and the trunks bending ever so slightly.

On and on, so much movement surrounding me, with me in the middle of it, standing in complete stillness, simply aware. It was in that moment that I felt the kind of relief Gusto had wished for me.

And with it came an amazing feeling of endless possibility. It was more than obvious that there were so many things going on behind the scenes that I wasn't yet aware of. Movement. Shifts. Confirmation that all I needed to do for the time being was hold on to the vision that made me feel alive. Give it my attention and know it was all in the works, all the while *letting go, letting go, letting go…*

I opened my eyes and turned to Gusto. He was smiling. He held on to the moment and then said, "When the time is right, you'll know just what to do. In the meantime, say to the unknowns, 'Don't worry. You can be unknown for now. It's okay with me.' There's beauty and there are gifts in just showing up like the pit. Speaking of that," he looked at the pits next to me, "did you eat them all?"

Laughing, I pointed to all the pits piled next to him.

He rolled his eyes, feigning exasperation. "Anyway," he said, "will you do this? Will you be still when it's time to be still, and then follow the little pushes when you hear them whispering to you?"

"I will."

I said goodbye and watched Gusto strut off toward the jungle. There wasn't a doubt in my mind he was going to find more mangos. And there wasn't a doubt that I would, at some point, again be facing the question of what to do when I didn't know what to do. So I took my flip-flop and wrote.

Until I hear a whisper or loud voice
inside telling me the next step, stand still
and let the how find its way to me.

When I feel moved to do something specific,
I'll have my full energy to do it. When that voice inside
talks to me or I feel a tiny push, I won't hesitate.
I'll follow it. In those inspired moments,
every time I lift my foot, I'll be bringing myself
closer to what I want.

15. The Volume of Uncertainty

My husband and I began talking out of necessity, to break the pain of silence. The conversations went in circles, taking us nowhere but back to the beginning, and neither of us understood the beginning. How could I have done what I did? What was wrong with me? The talk was exhausting for both of us; all of it felt charged and off-kilter and filled with static that only created more confusion.

We switched tactics, talking about only what needed to be addressed. Logistics of everyday living. Bills. The settlement money owed. What our refrigerator lacked. Bills. Survival. Bills. The basics. Back to where we had left off.

My husband was the first to bring up what we couldn't keep ignoring. Next to the coffee machine one morning. I didn't notice it until I pulled the coffee pot out. It was written on a napkin. *I need time. I don't know you anymore.*

I want to tell you I love you, because I know you need to hear it, but all I keep thinking is, Do I like her?

I wrote my response, went out to the patio where he was standing drinking his coffee, and handed it to him. *I don't like me either,* it said.

He read it and then gave the note right back to me, like he wanted nothing to do with it. "That's not fair," he said. "Don't do that. This can't be about *you.* You can't say something like that—something that asks for empathy. Do *not* ask that of me. Not now."

He was right; I knew it. "I don't know what to say."

He looked me in the eye for the first time in days. "Why did you do this to us?"

"I had no right to."

He turned away from me and threw the coffee mug on the cement. His voice breaking as unevenly as the mug had, he said, "Jesus Christ. Tell me something I don't already know."

I couldn't.

16. The Reminder to Remember

I had been thinking about my life and all the pieces of it. There were so many ingredients, so much I wanted to pull apart, mix together, fix, re-color, move about. I sat still with all of it for a long time until I felt moved to do something. Not surprisingly, it was a pull to go see Gusto that I felt moved by.

When I found him, he was building a sand sculpture. He waved me over and asked me to fill a pile of empty coconuts with water and bring them back to him so he could mix the water with the sand. I did as he asked, going back and forth to the water a few times, and then sat and watched as he shaped the sand into what looked like a thick totem pole a few feet high. He was completely engrossed in his work, and I loved watching his joy as he carved little details into his sculpture, replaced falling sand here and there, and added tiny shells and pebbles. And, of course, he whistled as he worked—a sign I had learned to take that Gusto was in his own world, not to be disturbed.

When he was finished, he stepped back, took a long look at it, and then turned to me and said, "So?"

"I love it." It was beautifully imperfect, raw and textured. And as fragile as I knew it was, there was something about it that appeared so strong and indestructible… until a moment later when a wave hit the shore, crawled up to the sculpture, and pulled it down, dragging the remnants back to the ocean.

Gusto had worked so hard—I knew his sculpture wouldn't last forever, but it was upsetting to see it get knocked down so quickly after he had completed it. When I looked at Gusto, however, he was smiling.

"What?" I said.

"Well, a little reminder, my Ophelia. What you most expect will be so."

"You expected your sculpture to get knocked down right after you finished it?"

"Ah-ha! Good question, my friend! No, I did not."

It didn't make any sense. "But you said that what you most expect will be so."

"Yes! You see, you're always creating. Either with purpose or without it. One or the other. I gave no care to whether or not it would fall. I'm an artist. Yes? Because I believe I'm an artist! When I came here to the beach this morning, I wanted to make a one-of-a-kind Gusto sculpture and have fun doing it. And I did! If I wanted to make art that would stand for a long, long time—perhaps days, perhaps years—would I have chosen to build it in the sand? *With* sand? And so close to the water? Do you see? What you intend leads to what you say and do. Intend something! Always. Because if you intend *nothing,* you let yourself be that tennis ball between other people and circumstances."

"I never want to feel like that again, but it doesn't seem natural to *always* be intending something. It actually feels complicated, almost disruptive to just living."

"Oh, but it's not! It's so very simple. Go right to the end. To how you want to feel. What is your intention? Is it joy? Love? Adventure? Simplicity? Abundance? Focus on the end result. Do it regularly, not obsessively. You can do it right now. What do you want to feel, right here and now? Do you know?"

I took a moment. "Yes." Three things immediately came to mind.

"Yes! Now imagine feeling it."

I imagined the feelings themselves, without thinking about what needed to happen in order for me to be able to feel them—only what they would feel like.

"Yes. So then, give attention to only that. Expect it. Allow it to be so. And it will. When I'm not sitting next to you asking questions, ask yourself. Always, my Ophelia. Ask yourself the questions you wish someone else would ask you. Then say what you want. Give your attention to the end, how you want to feel—and you'll take yourself to that feeling. If you focus on your desire for happiness and expect to be happy, you'll find only that which makes you happy. That's all you'll be able to see. That's all you'll be open to experiencing."

"But, Gusto, how do you know this is how things work? How do you know for sure?"

"The same way you know, my Ophelia."

But I didn't know…

I wasn't sure what he was getting at but was content to just leave it at that for the time being.

"Okay, then. Enough talk for now. Let's do something. Yes?"

"Absolutely." I loved Gusto's adventures. "What do you want to do?"

"You tell me. What do *you* want to do?"

I said the first thing that came to mind. "Let's swim."

"Delicious!"

So we ran down to the water. It was cold at first but then felt invigorating. We swam together for a while, duck-diving into the waves, and then once we were past the break where the water was calmer, I drifted off on my own, floating on my back. I let the saltwater buoy me, fully aware of its support as I stared up at the sky. There wasn't a cloud, not even a wisp. I felt merged with it; there was no separation between its clarity and my own.

That's when it hit me—when I remembered the three things I had imagined feeling. The three things I was feeling right then.

I didn't need to look over at Gusto. I knew he was smiling, too.

Later, when I went back to the beach, I wrote something on my flip-flop I never wanted to forget:

Along the way,
remember to decide how I want to feel.
Set that intention deliberately, giving my attention
to the end, how I want to feel in the result—
and I'll take myself to that feeling.

17. The Volume of Solitude

I kept waiting for that turning-point conversation, the one where my husband unleashed his anger, berated me, spilled out more than just a single sentence barely held together. But it didn't happen. He was quiet. As the days passed, it became obvious to me that the divide was something we wouldn't be working through together. He answered the phone when it rang. He read and handled the emails. He met with the lawyers, agreed on settlements. He met with our accountant. He called our daughter regularly to check in with her.

I took a job as a security guard at an art gallery, the night shift. The nineteen-year-old who had held the position for the last two years had just found out that his grades from the junior college were high enough for him to transfer to the state school he had been working toward getting into. The owner of the gallery needed a quick replacement, not because the gallery was in any actual danger of being vandalized or broken into, but because his insurance required twenty-four-hour security—whatever that looked like.

We needed the money, any amount, and I needed a reason to justify sleeping at odd hours during the day and not sharing our bed at night. Just as important, it would limit my contact with other people. I could go grocery shopping at night, on the way to work, or in the early morning when the store was just opening and the aisles were mostly empty.

It was dark out when I left for the first night of my new job. I put my pen back in my pocket and stuck one more Post-It note to the front door on my way out. *I'm sorry,* it said. There was one on the bathroom sink, on a framed photo of us hanging in the hallway, on a bottle of beer in the refrigerator, on his pillow on the bed that had become the most uncomfortable place in the house. I had gone through an entire stack of Post-It notes. I would have kept going if I hadn't run out. *I'm so, so, so sorry* the next one would have said.

When I came home, the Post-It notes were still there. They stayed put for a long time, until eventually, one by one they lost their stickiness and fell. I walked over them, around them, left them on the floor to collect dust.

18. The Matter of Understanding

The next time I went to see Gusto, he was in the jungle, chopping down bamboo. There was a huge pile of branches that he had already cut, so I asked him what he was working on.

"I'm not sure yet. Anyway, it's about time you showed up!" He stopped what he was doing and motioned for me to sit down with him.

"I've been doing it," I said.

"That's why you're smiling!"

"It feels so good to focus only on what I want and how I want to feel—just the end result, not worrying about all the hows. And here on the island, it manifests so quickly. It feels like I've tapped into a more magical way of living—and I love it! I hope that when I go back to my life, I can be patient enough, that I don't get frustrated or give up. Things there sometimes take a lot longer than I want them to. And a lot of times, it feels like I'm going nowhere and never will."

He smiled, leaned toward me, and whispered, "Do they really take a lot longer?"

"I think so. You don't?"

"Maybe they take longer than you want. Maybe not. Why do they happen so quickly here? Just a choice, Ophelia, like everything else. But let's save that for later.

"For now, let's say the timing of something bothers you because you don't understand it. You could believe things are working out perfectly and that the timing is perfect too—instead of believing that things aren't working just because you don't understand why they're happening the way they are and in the 'when' that they are. You see, it's like when I'm in my truck. When it's working, I sit in the driver's seat and let the car take me where I want to go. I don't think hard about it. I just go. I know it will take me. I expect it to. If my truck stops working when I'm driving, I don't jump out right away and start running in circles around the truck yelling, 'Why isn't this truck working! Something must be very wrong! This can't be good! What horrible, terrible timing!' Maybe instead I lift the hood to look underneath and slide under the truck to see if something's leaking. But, no, everything seems to be in order. Okay then. I don't know why my truck won't start. I want it to start, but it won't. I don't know what the reason is. Okay. But I believe—I know it's for a good reason. And so it is."

"But if you don't know the reason, what's stopping something from happening or working, you can't fix it. Don't you agree?"

"Maybe it wasn't actually broken! Or maybe I didn't find out why it wouldn't start until later—for a reason! Maybe a stranger came along and pointed out that the tank was empty—I had run out of gas. So we start talking, and that person ends up becoming someone important in my life. Maybe that person ends up being you! Maybe if I had not run out of gas, we would have never met. You decide whether things happen for a reason or not. And if you decide things happen for a reason, you get to decide whether the reason is in your favor or not. So, if you're in your truck and it stops suddenly and you don't know why, you can believe it's good for you or bad for you. Whatever you decide, it will be so."

It dawned on me that I had never seen Gusto in a truck and, more than that, couldn't possibly imagine him driving. Especially following the rules of the road. Not a chance. I had to ask. "Do you even have a truck?"

He started laughing and said, "Of course not! Crazy question, my friend. And I love crazy questions! But anyway, I know how a truck works."

"Okay, I was just wondering…"

"Wonder away! The matter of it is, you could do with wondering even more. But wonder up to possibilities instead of down to fear. You love so much to put labels on everything, as if each moment or phase could fit neatly in a box on a shelf—maybe even in order, yes? You look for a purpose, a meaning—always a meaning. No problem, my friend. But. When you don't see it yet, that's when you grow fear. It gets so big! Like a balloon you keep breathing into. Puff, puff—bigger and bigger! Then you think, *Oh, I must be doing something wrong!* Or, *Oh! This is bad! This couldn't possibly be something good!* Pop!

"There are times when you can't put the label on the box because the box doesn't exist yet. What you're in can't be contained. It's not time to make sense of it yet—there's just not enough information available to you. That's when you have a choice. Believe it's good or believe it's bad. As I said, whichever you decide, it will be so. It's really very simple. You see?"

"Yes." And I really did. In that moment, I saw how believing there was a favorable reason behind things I couldn't understand might change a lot—the experience itself being just one of those things.

"Yes, my friend. Yes. Anything is possible if you give the space for it. Even timing. Even reasons. It might just be that things are working out perfectly, better than you could even have imagined."

Gusto winked and added, "It might just be that you're living a beautifully colorful and textured life already— right now. But don't just take my word for it. Do an experiment. Try believing it. Try believing—without a doubt—that things are working out perfectly, better than you even hope they are. See what might happen if you were to decide you're already living a delicious life and you're already creating exactly what you want."

I figured the word "delicious" must have tugged at him because then off he went, abruptly ending the conversation, leaving me wondering if something he said might just be true. So I wrote it on my flip-flop.

It might just be that things are working out perfectly, including the timing of things, better than I could even have imagined. I'm going to wonder in that direction. A lot.

19. The Volume of Stories

My days became routine again. I came home from the gallery at 6:00 a.m., took a two-hour nap, and then spent the majority of the day uploading photos to different stock photo websites, unable to think of a better money-making option. I didn't want to go into our office anymore—it had become my husband's space—so I sat at the kitchen table on my computer, my eyes glazing over as I went through hundreds of folders of nature photos we had taken and tried to pick out the ones other people might want to look at, pictures that might be able to capture what someone else wanted to express through an ad, a cover, an illustration.

It was perfectly time-consuming and tedious, choosing the photos, editing them, plugging in the descriptions and keywords for each one, allowing me to ignore the fact that we had gone from making seven dollars a photo, with hundreds on order at a time, to seven cents a photo—*if* someone decided they wanted it among the millions of other photos competing to be chosen, if someone decided that it was worth something to them, that it would fulfill their need.

I took a nap at the end of the day and then left for the nightshift at 9:00 p.m. Every night at work, I roamed the gallery, looking for something to catch my eye, to talk to me, to tell me a story other than my own.

One night, I stood in front of a replica of Vermeer's painting, *Girl with a Pearl Earring.* I wanted to touch the soft blue of her headscarf, and I wondered why her face didn't have that softness. I stood there for a long time, looking into her eyes. And then it happened. I heard her speak. "You don't know me," she said, coveting her identity, and I felt like I had crossed some line, one I didn't belong crossing.

I turned and hurried away, without thinking. And that's when I found myself in the room that held the painting I had been avoiding. A bride. A groom. The celebration.

I leaned back against the wall, staring at the bride's face. The groom's. With tears streaming, I sank to the floor. I tried to come up with reasons, to understand why I had done what I had done, but nothing made it past a flickering of possible words to string together in my mind. There was no excuse.

I sat on the cold floor wishing it was colder, wishing it would numb me. I covered my face with my hands, crying into them, whispering angry words at myself. I pinched the skin on my hand, the palm, between my fingers, on top of my hand, moved up to my wrist, my arms, trying to distract myself from the pain inside. *Look at you. You have no right... When... Why...* I pinched harder. *You ruined everything... who do you think... disgusted... hate you...* Harder still, my nails digging deeper.

When I had nothing left to say to myself, I stood up, went into the bathroom, and splashed cold water on my face, careful to avoid looking in the mirror.

Knowing my shift would be over soon, I left the bathroom and did one more walk through, waiting for the man who had the next shift to arrive so I could sign my name beneath his on the employee in/out sheet and leave. There were no doors to be locked, but it didn't matter. I had already locked everything of value deep inside me.

20. The Time That It Is

I took Gusto's dare too seriously, and I went back to tell him I never wanted to do that again.

The sun was just beginning to rise, and Gusto was down in the water. He was tossing himself playfully into the waves, and as soon as he noticed me, he waved and called for me to join him. I waded out slowly at first and then dove in, swam past the breaking waves, and turned on my back, letting the water hold me up. With my ears submerged, I could hear the crackling sounds of the ocean and felt embraced by the symphony of life.

While the horizon was still pink, Gusto and I got out of the water and sat on the beach under the lifting moonlight and fading stars.

"So, Ophelia, did you find out what happens when you decide to believe everything's working out perfectly?"

"As much as I found out what happens when I think the opposite. They both work. You suggested I do an experiment." I smiled and said, "So I did."

"Ah-ha!"

"I let myself believe, and I mean really believe, that things weren't working out at all. And that was all I could see. Nothing felt like it was working. I got lost in the part of the jungle near the waterfalls, even though I know that area so well. I couldn't find any fruit to eat—and I was so hungry. One thing after another just seemed to go wrong; it felt like a downward spiral I couldn't step out of—until I finally decided to. I decided to believe that things were working out better than I could possibly imagine…"

"And?"

"Of course that's when I found the waterfalls and realized where I was. I even saw a rainbow there for the first time. Then I noticed that seaweed you told me about and tried it. You were right—it's delicious. And I realized it was a good thing I didn't find any fruit to eat, because my body definitely needed the seaweed to balance out all the acidic foods I've been eating lately. My body felt really happy." I smiled. "And so did I."

"Yes, my Ophelia. Yes. That's the beauty of a magnificent orchestra at work. Tell the universe what kind of music to play and then stand back and let it be the conductor."

I nodded. That's exactly what it felt like.

Looking up, Gusto pointed to the few visible stars and said, "Each one of them is distinct. Did you know that? Just like sunrises. No two are the same." He gazed at the expansive sky. "The gift of the stars, my friend, is that each one shines... in its own way."

He turned to me and said, "Maybe you'll make a promise to yourself."

I understood. "To shine," I said.

"Yes. In your own way. Because no two are the same."

His words ignited something in me—a combination of curiosity and excitement. I could tell he was thinking about something, and I was about to ask him if he was feeling that same excitement I was, but before I could ask, he said, "Are you hungry?"

So very Gusto. "Are you?"

"A crazy question! Thank you, my friend! Let's go."

And with that, we were off on a scavenger hunt around the island, searching for Gusto's favorite foods. Each time we came upon a new fruit, Gusto practically fell on his knees, acting as if it were the first time he had ever seen anything so fantastic, so unusual. And then, on cue, he would lean in as if to hear what the fruit was saying. Each fruit, of course, was speaking to him, beckoning him to taste it. So he did, sharing with me every time.

He found a durian and fell over laughing when he sliced it open and saw the look on my face. The odor was overwhelming. "That's why it's known as the stinky fruit!" he said, still laughing. "That's why it's even been banned in some places! But not here, my friend! Not here!" Then he whispered, "But did you also know it's an aphrodisiac? Ha-ha!"

He picked a carambola and immediately fell in love with the star that formed when he cross-sectioned it. We ate a rambutan, which I at first thought was a dark red puffer fish. Even though we were far from the water, I was starting to realize anything is possible with Gusto. We ate a soursop and a guava, until finally... Gusto was fully satisfied.

He found a mossy spot on the floor of the jungle, gathered some dry leaves for a pillow, and then lay down. Before drifting off to sleep, he looked up at me and said, "Who are you?"

Oh no, I thought. *What did we just eat?* The puffer-fish fruit immediately came to mind, and I braced myself for the hallucinations that were surely on their way.

But then he smiled. Four seconds later, he was snoring.

I watched him sleep. His question kept circling through my thoughts, over and around, again and again. *Who are you?*

When he woke up, he sat up and stretched, then jumped to his feet and asked, "Do you know what time it is?"

It was so unlike Gusto; he never cared about time. "I don't know," I said.

"You don't know?" He seemed genuinely surprised. "It's time to decide how it will be! Whether things will be difficult or whether they'll happen with ease. Who are you? Are you someone whose life is filled with heavy roadblocks, or do magical pathways lightly appear 'out of nowhere' for you? Because you get to decide. How do you want things to be?"

I had made a promise to myself to be totally honest, so I said, "Looking back, I think I wanted parts of my life to be difficult before—so I could see what I was made of, what I could handle."

"Yes. And now?"

"I want to believe in magic again—because that's the person I believe I really am. That's when I'm happy, and that's when I feel like I'm being most true to myself. I don't mind challenges, Gusto. I really do see value in them. But unnecessary friction and anxiety—I don't see purpose in that anymore."

"Yes! Yes!" Gusto did a little dance and told me he'd be right back.

A few minutes later, he handed me a coconut and a rock that looked like an arrowhead. "Are you thirsty?" he said. "Let's drink coconut milk! You do the honors."

I never thought I was hungry or thirsty until Gusto reminded me each time. I took the rock and jabbed at the coconut for a good long time, barely making a dent. When that didn't work, I got up and walked to a nearby rock that was far too big for me to carry and started banging the coconut against it. By now, I was somehow *really* thirsty. I stopped trying to crack the coconut on the rock when I noticed Gusto with his hands on his hips, shaking his head.

"What?"

He just looked at me.

"What?" I wanted him to say something, not just give me that disapproving look. I was feeling parched even though five minutes before I wasn't even thirsty; the suddenness of it put me on edge.

"What are you doing?" he asked.

I was about to answer the obvious, but then it hit me— what *he* was doing. And probably because of the deep thirst I was experiencing, it set me off. "What? You think this can be easy? But, Gusto… it's a coconut! Do you know how hard it is to open? I didn't decide that… it's already been decided. It's the property of a coconut! If you wanted me to practice doing something with ease, then maybe you should have given me something easier to do!"

He pointed to the top of a coco palm a few trees away where clusters of coconuts were dangling precariously. It had to be at least thirty feet high. "I couldn't have gotten you that coconut if I thought it would be difficult. Then it would have been. And then I would have wondered if maybe it was *too* difficult. And then it would have been.

"As you fall more and more in love with yourself and your life, there are going to be things you believe in, things you hope for, things you want to experience that other people will say are too hard or not possible. Or this or that. You have to decide whether or not what other people think—and what you may have thought before— is true. You choose: my life is fun and flows, or—my life is very difficult, and I have so many things in the way. What you decide will be so.

"So then, my friend. You really should hear me. Yes? How will it be? It's up to you."

I looked at him, into his eyes, and saw my reflection. I didn't like what I was looking at; I wanted to soften it. I gently but firmly assured myself that I could easily quench the thirst I was experiencing, and as I did that, the thirst immediately lessened, demanding far less attention from me, and then every thought but one disappeared. The only one left was *ease*. I let go of every rational reason suggesting that it was impossible for me to open the coconut with just the small rock. I sat down. Then, closing my eyes and following my gut instinct, I slowly ran my hands over and around the coconut. I imagined that I had never seen a coconut, that I had never been taught anything about the coconut. I just felt the rough and bristly texture, introducing myself to it with the touch of my fingers.

Then I felt it. A soft spot.

With my eyes still closed, I began slowly digging into the soft spot of the coconut, twisting the rock in deeper as I focused on one thing only: believing it could happen with ease.

It split open, and the coconut's milk poured out over my hands. That's when I realized I was no longer thirsty. I sat there for a moment taking in what had just happened, realizing that what I was so sure was impossible had become possible. I ran my hand along the inside of one end of the coconut, caressing its smooth skin. As I circled my fingers around the inside of the other half, I noticed it wasn't nearly as smooth. I followed the crevices with my fingertips and then opened my eyes and saw words etched into the stark white of the inside of the second half:

Fearlessly decide.

Gusto smiled. "Nothing else to say, my friend."

He nodded, letting me know we would meet again soon, and I handed him the coconut, which he gladly accepted. When he was gone, I wrote what I thought might be the last words that would fit on my left flip-flop.

Fearlessly decide.

And then I found a little more space and added:

And it will be so.

21. The Volume of the Past

While looking through computer files for more photos to submit to the stock photo websites, I came across an old folder titled "We Are." Even before clicking to open the folder, I knew what was there. Years back, we had started to take pictures for an art piece we wanted to create together. We were going to take a large, square piece of pine, give it a rustic painted look, and then layer it with things showing who we were, my husband and daughter and me, and who we wanted to be together.

The plan was to hang it with two pieces of heavy twine, just a few inches away from the wall so that it had room to sway a little, to allow movement. We would layer it with our daughter's drawings, notes we had written each other over the years, wax dripping from colored candles, our favorite quotes, used maps, album covers, random photos that we felt particularly drawn to for whatever reason—a picture of an old man fishing, hands in the process of building something, bare feet propped up by a fire, a garden with seventeen kinds of spices growing, a pile of books that would one day be read and discussed, fenceless land, a palm tree, a close-up of my husband's eyes when he was laughing, our daughter's, mine, a fountain, a stream, a lake, so much water, hiking boots and flip-flops... layers and layers of a life lived. We had found miniature colored-glass jars to fit over the bulbs on a strand of Christmas lights—homemade light fixtures to illuminate the art piece at random points. My husband had borrowed a tool from a friend so he could cut precise holes in the wood, here and there, and then we could insert each bulb from the string of lights through the back of the wood. He had gotten advice about what kind of glue would be best to adhere the colored-glass covers over each bulb poking through.

I stared at the contents of the folder on the computer, remembering it all, and for the flicker of a moment, it all felt possible again. Then I looked at the clock at the bottom corner of the screen and realized it was time to leave. I remembered the reality that was ours now.

As I drove to the gallery, I thought about the friends we had shared our plan with. *Was it three years ago?* I wondered. *Four?* I wasn't sure. We were out at dinner, and unable to contain my excitement, I had waited until just after we ordered. Then I told them all about it, the art piece we had envisioned and how we had gone to the hardware store the day before and gotten the rest of the supplies we needed. All the photographs were printed, and all the other personal pieces, everything was in stacks and piles, ready to be assembled. When I had finished, our friends looked at each other and then back at us, and the husband, trying too hard to sound gentle, broke the awkward silence and said, "It's not a bad idea. It's just a little… I don't know." He looked at his wife. "Corny?" She gave that look, like she was afraid that, yes, she had to agree. Hesitantly so, but still, yes, she had to agree.

Why did my husband and I move right on to other conversation topics with them, engaging as if any of us meant anything we were saying? Why did my husband keep avoiding the eye contact I was trying to make with him? Why did I stop looking at him? Why did we get together with that couple again? And again and again? I wished my husband and I had gotten up from the table right then, in the instant they took a hammer to our idea, looked at us with pity. I wished we had left the restaurant, went straight to the friend's house where our daughter was and picked her up, went home to our garage where all the supplies were sitting, before they collected dust. I wished we had stayed up all night, the three of us, defining our life and creating our future together. I wished we had done what we were excited about doing, hung it up on the wall and looked at it and talked about it and added to it every day. I wished we hadn't eventually piled other things, useless things, on top of the stacks of maps and photos and notes and drawings and our future in the garage. I wished I hadn't forgotten about it. I wished my husband hadn't. It wasn't our daughter's job to remember. It was ours. Mine and my husband's—equally.

As I pulled into the parking lot of the gallery, I realized that it was sometime after we had a child that my husband and I began looking less and less to each other for validation of our ideas and hopes and dreams, that we started depending on other people's perceptions of what was worthy of our time and energy and thoughts and efforts. Some who knew us well. Some who didn't know us at all. Especially as our daughter grew up, we listened closer, leaned in to garner every word as if, because we had a child now, we could no longer decide on our own.

We used to talk about carpentry, the art of it. My husband had a friend, the one he borrowed tools from, who made specialty furniture, and my husband loved stopping by to help him. "There are eyes in every piece of wood," my husband used to say. "I want to see them all." He learned a lot from his friend, and we talked about his dream of making one-of-a-kind pieces of furniture with rustic character—inspired, useful, lasting. He was serious about the possibility, and so was I. He was fully engaged whenever I talked about maybe someday becoming a student again. I wanted that interaction with other people, the two-way teaching and talking and figuring things out together, an environment all about learning, so much more than the subject itself. I had no idea what I wanted to learn, but it never felt like an obstacle, just something that would eventually figure itself out. We talked about living abroad. Iceland, Costa Rica, the Philippines. We felt attracted to a list of changing places, though we had never been to them before. Could we do a few months there? Figure it out? We believed we could. We talked about getting bicycles and riding them on cobblestone streets, making croissants from scratch, milking a cow, even if just once.

We used to talk about our ideas and dreams, not like they were farfetched fantasies, but very real possibilities. And then we slowly tuned out the people who said "Do it" and meant it, like their voices were scratches on a record, and we tossed the B-sides in a drawer with a key we dropped along the way, and instead we started listening to what other people voiced with authority, experience to back it up. We heard the word *realistic* again and again, a question in a cacophony of voices, and then we started reassigning what was real.

The security guard whose shift ended as mine began was standing at the gallery entrance, waiting for me. I got out of the car and did my best not to slam the door.

22. Letting Go of What is Not Yours

Gusto greeted me at our spot and said, "Let's take a walk."

We began walking down the stretch of beach. Though there were no signs of life, not even the pipers or crabs we had grown accustomed to, it didn't feel deserted. In fact, I felt like we weren't alone at all.

We walked in silence until Gusto said, "It's time for another decision—to decide what's true and what is not."

I knew right away what this was about. Since our last conversation, I had given a lot of thought to the different people in my life. I realized that one of my biggest challenges to being who I know I am would be facing who other people think I am. Not all, but some. A few whose opinions really mattered to me. I had decided who I was, but I wasn't fearless in my decision. Not yet anyway. And at times, I felt a little terrified that certain other people might be right—about me, about everything.

Gusto nodded and said, "Ophelia, no one—look into my eyes—*no one* knows the certain truth about you except you. Hear what people have to say. But never stop there. Always take it one step further. Step away into silence and go into your heart. Ask yourself just one question: *Do I feel truth in that?* Again, honesty will take you everywhere you need to go. If you hear that you're too sensitive, go into your heart and feel if that's true. If it isn't, release it. It's that simple. If it is, okay then. So now you deal with that truth. Do I want to be very sensitive? Is it good or bad? Or neither. Or both. If someone tells you that you're ridiculous, again, feel in your heart whether or not it's true. *Do I feel truth in that?* If not, dismiss it. Let it fall away from you like a handful of sand. If it's true, ask yourself: Is it good or bad? Or neither or both? Do I want to be ridiculous?"

"I think I do," I said.

Gusto stopped and picked up a conch shell. He turned it over a few times, examining it closely. Then he looked at me and said, "Hold this to your ear; it will talk to you. It will repeat what other people, mostly well-meaning, have said to you about you. It will tell you what other people believe is realistic or possible for you. Here, try."

I shook my head. "I don't want to."

"It's not so difficult or scary. You're brave. You can face anything! Feel that. In order to be who you are and fall in love with life, you need to let go of any thoughts about you that don't feel true. Things other people have said to you, labels you decided to believe, limits you chose to accept. Some will feel true to you; some will not. It's simply about holding on to what's true and letting go of what isn't. Listen to the words and notice how you feel. True? Not true? You'll *feel* it. Here." He scooted next to me. "I'll listen with you."

"Okay," I said. I took the shell and held it to my ear. Gusto leaned in on the other side, and we listened.

First, I heard nothing. Then, like little fireworks popping one after another, I heard them all. One by one. Everything I had ever heard or felt or been taught about me. Everything I had ever said or believed about myself. They came quickly—each word, every phrase—but my heart, somehow not at all overwhelmed, immediately knew what to do with every one of them. My head's job was to listen to the rapid firing of words; my heart's job was to tell me the truth of each one. I didn't need time to think about anything, to analyze or justify or defend or deny. I simply listened, feeling my heart's response.

Gusto put his head down, covered his face with his hands, and started shaking. I had never seen him cry.

Then I heard it. His laughter escaping. He was doubled over, laughing and laughing.

"What is it?" I asked, starting to laugh too.

"Did you hear what someone said about me!" He could barely get the words out, he was laughing so hard now. "A... a... *a quacking duck!*" The tears were streaming down his face. "If I believed that, I'd start waddling...

then grow a beak… then start shaking my feathers! Can you imagine!"

I was starting to, and it had me laughing almost as hard as he was.

He gathered himself, shook his head, and put his arm around my shoulder. "I'm not a duck! You see?"

"I do."

"Okay, so of all that you heard, certain words stood out for you. Yes? Tell me."

I explained how a lot of the words were really positive, compliments—*spirited, attentive, ambitious,* and more—and it felt good to acknowledge those things about myself. It felt important. Another was a criticism that hit hard—*selfish*—and it felt true. Being honest with myself about it was liberating. And more than that, the word felt like an observation of certain choices I had made in the past, not a permanent character trait I was stuck with. There was relief in the awareness that if I didn't want that word to describe me, I could make different choices. Finally, the last word that stood out was in huge letters, much bigger than the rest. It was a negative one. *Hopeless.* It was a tough one because it didn't feel true—it actually felt destructive—but it was so ingrained in my perception of myself, I wasn't sure how to release myself from its grip.

Gusto took my hand and led me down to the water's edge.

The waves were violently crashing and then shrinking and losing momentum as they approached our feet. "Let the word go, my friend. The ocean is powerful; let the waves take that word that doesn't feel true and turn it inside out until it's just individual letters again, no longer a word. Then you can arrange the letters in a new way, dropping some, adding others, however you want to, in a way that feels true."

A wave crawled toward me, and as it pulled at my feet, making me sink into the wet sand, I gave the word to the ocean. I watched the blue-green water take *hopeless* away and dismantle it, turning it inside out, scattering the letters. I couldn't see where they went, but the word no longer felt like a part of me. And in that moment, I felt younger, wiser, and freer than I'd ever felt. I felt more creative, more thoughtful, more successful, more important, more beautiful than I had ever remembered feeling. I silently thanked the ocean for helping to free me.

After a few minutes, Gusto pointed to a pelican gliding right above the water about twenty feet in front of us, the first we had seen since we started on our walk. "You'll know you're free of any thought or belief that's held you down when you can climb up on that pelican's back without it even noticing, soaring weightlessly through the air."

I focused on the pelican as it hovered above a building wave, a few inches over the rising crest. In the clarity of the wave before it broke, right beneath the pelican, I saw the letters the ocean had pulled apart—*h* and *o* and *p* and *e* and *l* and *e* and *s* and *s*.

The last three letters tumbled out of view, leaving *h* and *o* and *p* and *e*—and a lingering *l*. I watched as the letters rearranged themselves, coming together as *o* and *p* and *h* and *e*. And then the *l* stopped lingering, as if it had suddenly found a purpose, and slid over so that it followed the *e*. From underneath, *a* and *i* rose to the crest, joining, placing themselves where they belonged until, all together, they spelled out something new. *O* and *p* and *h* and e and l and *i* and *a*. I said it out loud. "Ophelia."

I am not hopeless. I am Ophelia.

I took my name inside of me. I embraced my essence.

And then, in a stunning show of light, though the wave came crashing down, *Ophelia* was still intact, unbroken, floating on the surface of the water.

Gusto smiled. "You have just one job, in the whole of your life. To be true to yourself."

"I like that." I could picture myself on the pelican. It was easy to climb on. The pelican took off, soaring high above the ocean.

"Yes… *you* get to decide who you are," Gusto said. "If you observe people, you'll notice something: the happiest people are the ones who are free. They're free of that heavy bag filled with everyone else's definitions and rules and judgments. They dropped that bag off somewhere along the way. Emptied it out or just left it where they found it. They know who they are. They have their own rules. And no matter what's going on in their life, they're at peace, a peace that can't be broken."

The pelican swooped low, glided around in a circle, and then coasted close to where the water held hands with the beach. As if I were riding it, I felt its movement inside me.

"Your job, Ophelia, is to be who you are and shape your life into one *you* fall in love with. It can be simpler just to set out on the road that was paved for you by other people's thoughts. And there may be a strong temptation to believe that everyone else knows more than you do about who you are and what your life should look like. But, my friend, do you hear me quacking right now? Do you see me waddling?"

I laughed, and that made him smile.

"You're your greatest source of wisdom and knowing. No one else. You can't give it away and let someone else decide for you. Remember that… and you'll see me soon. Yes?"

"Yes."

And with that, he made his way to the jungle behind us. My attention though was on the pelican that had glided toward me and landed, right where Gusto had been.

As I stood looking at the ocean, the pelican silently beside me, I smiled. I knew that every moment between now and the next time I saw Gusto, he would be having more fun than anyone would think possible, being foolishly optimistic according to some people, unrealistically happy according to others. He would continually create a life he was in love with. And he wouldn't give it a second thought.

I took my other flip-flop, the blank one, and wrote a reminder to myself in big letters.

*No one but me can decide who I am,
what I'm capable of, and what my life should look like.
I'm embracing that honor.*

23. The Volume of Reasons

When I arrived home in the morning from the gallery, my husband was sitting at the table in the kitchen. He looked worn and old.

"We need to talk," he said.

I sat down across from him and waited for him to begin.

"I can't do this anymore."

"Neither can I."

He took a deep breath the way he does when he's spent a long time rehearsing what he's about to say. "We've been married for twenty years, and until recently, you were always the love of my life. I have hope, some hope, that we can make it through this... I'm trying to... but I need to understand—things like why we're probably going to lose this house. We have no friends anymore. Can you explain that to me? How is it that you and I, two people who were once in love, can barely look at each other? I need to understand." He shook his head. "I need to understand why you destroyed our business."

"I haven't been happy… *we* haven't been happy. I know that's not an excuse, but if you want a reason, that's the one I have to give you." I sounded like a robot. I hated the tone of my voice and every word I had just said.

He was looking at me, waiting. I forced myself to go on. "I could explain more, but it feels wrong to, like I'm somehow okay with it because there's a way to explain it. It wasn't okay. It's not understandable. That's the bottom line. I know you deserve more of an explanation, I really do, but there is no good one."

"No. That won't cut it anymore. This is one of those crossroads we used to talk about. I can't move forward without knowing. Why did you do it, Ophelia? Why didn't you take a *single* picture of the bride or groom?" It had taken him five weeks to ask me that question.

"I know why I did it, but I don't want to say it out loud. Giving it a voice… it makes it sound like I have an excuse. Haven't you ever felt so horrible about something that you refused to name a reason for what you did? Because you were afraid that if you named the reason, then the next step would be pretending it was a good reason? And then before you knew it, you would have forgiven your-self for something that was never—*will* never—be okay? Don't you see? The only reason you want me to tell you is because you're hoping it'll help you forgive me. And I can't help you do that."

He took a deep breath and then looked down at his hands in his lap. "Ophelia, you're the *only* one who can explain this. *The only one.* You need to help me understand. You need to make this right. I don't know how you'll do it, but it needs to happen." He looked up at me. *"You have to fix this."*

I leaned forward. "I can't even *fix* me." Anger surged through me. "Why did you let me destroy everything?"

"What? Why did I *let* you?"

"Yes. *You.* Why didn't you tell anyone it was my fault there were no pictures of the bride and groom? Call it a nervous breakdown or say I had lost it or whatever. Why did you take it on as if you'd done it? Why did you watch the business fall apart and not stop it? It didn't have to. You could have stopped it. You *know* that. Why didn't you? Why didn't you cut me out of it? Why haven't you left me? Divorced me? *Why are you still here?* Did some part of you want everything to fall apart? Was some part of you okay with that? Because if that's the truth, I need to know. Is there a part of you—*any* part of you—that's actually relieved even though it's the last thing you're supposed to feel right now? I need to know I'm not crazy, that there's a reason you haven't left, that there's a reason you let us lose everything, that there's a reason you're still here after what I did. I need to know why you didn't save yourself from this, why you still haven't saved yourself from *me.*"

He stood up. "I need some air."

24. The Dance of the Flame

Gusto was waiting for me at our spot on the beach, adding sticks to a small bonfire. The yellow-orange flames looked like miniature figures dancing against the backdrop of the black night sky. Pleased with the fire, Gusto wrapped himself in a woven blanket and started snacking on kiwi. I sat down next to him and took the other blanket. Underneath was a bowl carved from a coconut, filled with my very own kiwi slices.

I looked at Gusto and said what I had been thinking about since seeing him last. "I'm so in love with who you are, Gusto. Your passion for life. Your ability to trust. Your determination to have fun. The way you so easily live—with your head in the clouds. I'm a little worried about being able to do that consistently when I go back; I hope I know how to keep you alive in me." I knew the time was approaching for me to leave the island; I could feel it and everything it stirred in me.

Gusto put his hands behind his back and said, "Pick a hand."

I pointed to his left side. "That one."

"Lucky you!" He brought his hand from behind his back and gently opened it. A firefly with a cobalt blue tail fluttered its wings in his palm. It looked at me, and maybe I was tired and imagining things, but I thought it winked. Then it flapped its wings and flew off.

"The firefly can just be the firefly," Gusto said. "Lucky firefly. Lucky you."

I wasn't sure how to respond.

"You don't have to be anything else here," he said. "Just you. Sometimes that's the place you need to go to. Yes?"

"Yes."

"It's time to look into the fire and see nothing but the flames. Time to move deeper into who you are. It's time to see it all."

He rubbed his hands together and then placed them a few inches in front of the fire. "Nighttime beauty. Nothing like it."

Gusto smiled, and I knew he had something special in mind. He put his warm hands on my face and said, "Magnificence... that's what it's time to see."

He threw his arms into the air and said, "Magnificence. I'm Gusto the Magnificent. I know that. And you're magnificent, too—exactly as you are. To know that, and to celebrate all of who you are—that's how you keep your Gusto alive."

He got up and, taking his blanket with him, moved to the other side so that the fire danced between us. He looked at me through the flying sparks and waving flames. "So then," he said. "Ask yourself the simple question: *Who am I?* Isn't that what you wish others would ask you? Do you remember when I asked you before? Who are you, Ophelia? Ask yourself. Ask it again and again. Not thinking about it, just allowing the answers to show up. Ask from your heart. Ask from your heart."

He took a deep breath and closed his eyes. I did the same.

Who am I?...

Who am I?...

I realized I had never asked the question before, not like this. Not from my heart. And not without expectations.

Who am I?

At first, all I saw were the dancing flames I had just closed my eyes to.

Then...

Who am I?

Slowly, slowly, the answers began to emerge. They continued surfacing for an entire minute, a whole hour—I have no idea. There was no time.

* * *

When I opened my eyes, I was crying. I tried to explain it to Gusto, but I couldn't.

He nodded and said, "There are no words for it, my friend."

There weren't, but I wanted to express something so I would remember.

And so I began, telling him through the crackling fire between us.

I am Ophelia.

I create. I choose. I'm the architect of my life. I'm the builder. I have all the tools I need. I have dreams. I remember. I reach for the star that calls to me. I'm my own star. I shine. I have a voice. I listen. I have meaning. I give meaning.

I'm limitless. I'm life. I'm love.

I am hope.

I am Ophelia.

He closed his eyes and nodded. When he opened his eyes, they were filled with happy tears.

Gusto came over next to me, put his arm around me, and said, "Yes, Ophelia. You're magnificent. Hold on to who you are. Everything moves out from that point— from knowing who you are: every thought you choose to build, every word you speak, every decision you make, and every action you put in motion. It's the center.

"Let it speak to you. No matter where you are or what you're doing or who's standing next to you."

Gusto leaned forward, blew once, and a wind came from somewhere far away, taking the sparks with it as the fire went out. Gusto was gone, and I sat with the realization that I could feel the spark inside me dancing the dance of the blue-orange flames.

Before going to sleep that night, I wrote another note.

I am Ophelia. That's the starting point of everything. And the journey. And the destination.

My writing was getting bigger—as if my hand had a say of its own—and I knew it wouldn't be long until I ran out of space on my second flip-flop. But it didn't bother me. I was filled with a peace that couldn't be broken, that needed nothing, not even the words I had just written. They were already a part of me.

25. The Volume of Seeing

I was still sitting at the kitchen table an hour after my husband left. He needed air, he had said.

Finally, I took my pen out of my pocket, got up, and found some paper in the drawer. I wrote a letter to the bride. Apologizing. Taking responsibility.

What I didn't say in my letter was why I had purposely done what I did.

I didn't tell her that when I was taking the pictures while she was getting ready—pictures I later deleted— and the best man came and knocked on her partially open door, I saw their eye contact. I didn't tell her that I felt the electricity of the moment, that as women, these things can't be hidden from us. I didn't tell her that I knew exactly why she asked me to leave, saying she just needed some time alone with him. I didn't tell her that it had finally made sense to me, the strange excuses she had given her mother and sisters and bridesmaids, telling them why she and I needed a private photo shoot while she was getting ready. I didn't tell her that I wasn't the fool she took me to be.

I didn't tell her because I knew that no matter what I saw, I was there to take pictures of what they wanted to see.

I didn't tell her that I couldn't stand contributing to anything pretend anymore, adding to all that was already fake. That the pictures would have been lies. That my own life was starting to look like a collection of framed perfect photos, taken out of context, that the thoughts and feelings inside me were often so far from what a snapshot suggested to an outside observer. I didn't tell her that all the Photoshopping was sucking the life out of me because none of it was raw or real.

I told her only that I had no right to do what I had done. And that I was extremely sorry.

When I came back from the post office, the letter sent, my husband had returned from wherever he went. He started talking as soon as I walked in the door.

"You wanted to know if I'm relieved?" he said. "No. I'm not. There's no relief in this. This isn't how it had to happen, and you had no right to put me in this position. Yes, I've always wanted more for us, and I knew we wouldn't be photographers forever. I know we always talked about doing a lot of other things, not just one thing our whole life, and yes, I could feel things getting old. *Of course* I knew it wasn't the way it used to be. But you didn't have to destroy it all to get my attention. That was an insult. What you did was wrong—to me, to our daughter, to the couple and their families and their friends. And no, there's no relief in being wronged—or being married to the person who wronged so many people.

"Now, you want to know why I didn't stop it all from falling apart? Because it had *already* fallen apart—us, you and me. You said it yourself: we weren't happy. I wasn't looking at the business falling apart. Do you really think that's what my focus was on? Saving the business? How could I possibly even think about that with so many other questions right in front of me—questions about *us*. You want to know why I haven't left you? Because I'm terrified of what I know—that if I leave you, if I let go of us, I'll be walking away from the best thing that ever happened to me. But I don't know how to fix us, and it feels like as long as we're broken, nothing will ever work."

"I—"

"No. Don't say anything. Not yet. I don't need you to answer. I need you to think about something. I need you to think about the fact that I really don't know how to come back together with you. It's not that I don't want to or am refusing to. I don't know *how* to. I don't know how to get past the anger. I don't know how to forgive you. I can't even *see* you anymore, the you I once knew. In fact, I honestly don't know how to see you as anyone other than the most hopelessly selfish person I've ever met. I need you to show me how to see *anything* other than that."

26. The Matter of Connectedness

Instead of one of our usual spots on the beach, Gusto picked a space carpeted with small rocks, each one different, so many colors and textures. We invented names for them, building our stories and deciding which sea creatures they had left behind to take a nap on the beach and soak up the sun.

There was the round, yellow-speckled rock that we decided was the "pearl that wasn't," discovered when a lobster pried open an oyster shell. They soon became the kind of friends that last. The rock was now on a journey to find a one-of-a-kind thank-you gift for the lobster. After all, it was the lobster that had opened the oyster shell and released the rock into a whole new world, offering it a different identity. It was no longer the pearl that wasn't.

And there was the long, algae-covered rock that we decided broke away from the wall of a cave deep in the ocean, intent on searching for its twin it believed was somewhere on the wall of another cave. It had heard from a seahorse that a similar-looking rock had headed for the shore. And so it had followed that lead.

We created story upon story.

Then Gusto got on his knees and whistled away, connecting each of the rocks, creating a circular spiral in the sand. When it was almost complete, he reached to his side and picked up what had been distracting me, pulling at my attention the entire time we had been talking. I saw the rust-colored starfish in Gusto's hand, and I knew what he was going to do.

"Ah, yes. The finishing touch," he said, about to place it in the center of the spiral.

"Don't," I said.

He looked at me.

"Don't, Gusto. I'm serious." He created using symbols, yet being transparent was his modus operandi. It was obvious that, for him, the starfish symbolized me. And putting it in the center of the spiral would, sooner than I was ready for, manifest as me back in the center of my life, surrounded by all the people in it.

"It's almost time," he said.

"No."

"But, Ophelia…" He started lowering his hand.

"Please don't. Please, *please* don't."

He pulled his hand back, put the starfish in his pocket. "Talk to me."

Elizabeth Day

"It's just that I've finally remembered who I am—all of it. And I don't want to forget. I'm so scared of immersing myself in my old life again. In the past, too often I tried to be someone other than who I was. There were times when I tried to adjust other people's stories to fit better with mine, or I adjusted my story to blend better with theirs. The need to feel connected took over. And whenever I did that, I disconnected from the true me. I wasn't allowing the distinctions between me and other people; I wasn't choosing to simply be okay with them. Now that I've remembered who I am, I'm afraid of stories other than the one I'm living on the island right now with you; I didn't know how to co-exist with them. I'm afraid of them slowly, eventually smothering the flame that's now—*finally*—dancing inside me again."

It was such a relief to admit the truth, how I felt, and I was surprised by the surge of emotion that followed.

"Good," Gusto said. "Good. Take your time. I'll be back."

I put my head in my hands and let myself feel the deep sadness that was beneath all the fears I had just released. I cried. And cried and cried. I wanted to do better, so much better. With everyone, especially my husband and daughter. At the same time, I didn't want to sacrifice who I had become.

* * *

Sometime later, I took a deep breath and opened my eyes. I saw Gusto's bare feet in the sand right in front of me.

I lifted my head and looked up at him, grateful to have him back. He was standing there with his hand out to me, holding a pomegranate.

"I brought you this," he said, kneeling down in front of me. "Because a pomegranate is a pomegranate."

He sliced it in half, and royal red juice slowly spilled out. "Look at this! Have you ever seen anything like it? Exquisite!" He pulled out a seed, held it in front of him, and then presented it to himself, saying, "Little impeccable seed. Yes." Then he tasted it, his eyes growing wide with delight.

Gusto pulled out a few seeds for me, moved from kneeling to a sitting position, and said, "You know something? There are those who remind you that you have a voice and encourage you to sing. And there are those who suggest you have a voice they can barely hear." He shrugged. "Don't try to make a pomegranate a pitaya. It doesn't work. Keep it simple, my friend. Just pay attention to your feelings and recognize which is which.

"When you try to cause a shift in someone's story— any shift—pushing to make them or their story different in some way, it doesn't leave you feeling good, does it?"

"No, it doesn't." I had been there before, though it was often disguised as other things.

"No. Because you cannot control anyone but you. And thank all the fruit on this island for that! So instead of trying to force a shift in someone else, step back and page through your own story that's always in the making. What shift can you make to bring about what it is you truly want—the real reason behind the curtain of wanting to adjust someone else's story. What does *your* story need? More wisdom? More generosity? More forgiveness? More strength? More trust? More courage?"

Gusto reached into his pocket, took out the starfish, and placed it in my hand.

"Now I'll tell you her story. Yes?"

I nodded.

"That's an adventurous starfish in your hand, my Ophelia. She has such big ideas about her life. So one day she was floating near the surface, feeling happy, when suddenly a swordfish came gliding through the water and ran right into her. The starfish thought it was an accident. But no, the swordfish was an angry fish, in a bad mood that day. For the next while, the starfish just kept getting poked and tossed around by the swordfish. It took some time, but finally she remembered, *I'm a starfish. I'm not a toy for a swordfish.* So she stopped the game with the swordfish. She remembered that she could point herself in any direction, whenever she wanted to, and so right then and there, she focused all her attention on one of her lower arms and directed herself down to the peace of lower waters, out of reach of the swordfish.

"You see, Ophelia, though you can't control someone else's story, you always have complete say over yours. No interaction is neutral. Each person affects the other in some way or another. Positive or negative. Like a dash of salt or pepper spices a mango. Each interaction makes your life taste better or worse. One or the other. So keep it simple."

"And if it's negative?" I said. "And someone I care about? What do I do with it?"

"Remember your you-ness just as the starfish remembered who she was and the different directions she could take herself. Your you-ness will always tell you how to respond in any situation—what *your* story needs in that moment."

"I haven't always known though. Sometimes I feel like I can't see clearly enough to know."

Gusto seemed to consider that for a moment. "Okay then. Yes. If the waters have become too muddy and thick, imagine there's a rope stretched between you and that person. They're pulling on their end of the rope; you're holding the other end in your hands, pulling just as hard. Tug, tug. Both of you. No problem! They can't pull at you if you let go of your end of the rope. Let go with love. Remember, gratitude makes it possible to move forward. Bitterness and resentment hold you back, keep you holding on to the rope—even if it's with just one hand. A single finger. Do you see? Let go of your end of the rope."

"But what if I lose them?"

"You may find that rather than losing them, you find them. And you find yourself again. Letting go of the rope changes the dynamic of your relationship to that person; it will *loosen* what has been too tight. There will be no more tugging. Now, there is space. Ahhh… And now, anything is possible. Space is sometimes the best gift you can give. Sometimes it's physical space… but more often, it's other kinds of space. The space for that person to be who they are. And the space for you to be who you are."

I nodded. I understood.

"So then, I'll finish the story about that starfish in your hand. Let's go back in time. Before it met the sword-fish. One day while sitting on the ocean floor, the star-fish noticed a long strand of dark green seaweed waving back and forth. *Hmm,* the starfish thought. *I want to do that, too. And I wonder if the seaweed knows how many directions it can wave in. So much more than just back and forth.* So the starfish set about learning how to let the tides roll her here and there until she felt the motion of waving, just like she had seen the seaweed do. She got so into it, she could even use all five of her arms to wave in any direction at once! And during that time, she taught the seaweed how to spring forward, reach up, dip down, push off to the side, and somersault back. The seaweed had no idea there were so many directions for it to go in; it was grateful to the starfish for showing so many possibilities. The starfish and the seaweed understood the matter of fun together and learned many things from each other. But before long, the tides had moved the star-fish far away, and it couldn't see the seaweed anymore.

"Eventually, the starfish noticed a bright yellow coral just a few feet away. *Ohhh,* she thought. *Look how calm and still that coral is.* In their time together, the coral taught the starfish how to calm each of her five arms and finally her center so that she could experience stillness. The starfish, not even realizing the difference she was about to make, one day told the coral something it had never known—that there was a sun high above the depths of the ocean and that the coral brought that same golden light into what would otherwise be darkness. After that, every time the coral thought of itself, it felt radiant.

"It was while practicing stillness that the starfish eventually floated up to the surface of water, soon becoming the swordfish's target. After she had put space between herself and the swordfish, she knew she was tired and needed rest. She needed to just *be* for a while. No agenda. To just see what happened next. So she let the ocean carry her to the shore, one wave after another, right here to you."

I looked at the starfish, running my fingers over each of its arms.

"Yes. Look closely," Gusto said. "What do you see?"

I could see them so clearly. "The strand of seaweed. The coral. The sun. The waves."

"And the swordfish?"

I looked deep into the starfish. "Barely a trace."

Gusto smiled. "Magnificence," he said. "I'll be right back."

He didn't need to tell me where he was going.

* * *

Gusto came back with two mangos and two husks filled with coconut water. Handing me one of each, he said, "Ready?"

I was ready for all of it—the mango, the coconut water, and for him to go on.

He explained, "Every person that steps into your life does so for a reason, just as you walk into their life for a reason. Let other people be who they are, and you— be who you are. And then make choices. Give thought and attention not to those who turn down the volume on your voice but to the people who inspire your song."

"What if it's not possible to be with them—some of those people who bring out who I really am?"

"Time doesn't separate you. Nor does distance or circumstance. You could feel the presence of the seaweed, the coral, the rolling waves, the sun—all in the starfish. You could *see* them in her! She chose to keep their energy connected."

One person after another came to mind then, and Gusto and I talked about each one. Some had been in my life for as long as I could remember. Others had passed in and out with the seasons. They were all important, and I felt grateful for them, filled with a love that I struggled to express.

"Sometimes words aren't needed," Gusto said. "Sit in the power of that love. Breathe it in. Be absorbed by it. Then, when you feel complete with it, send that love to them. They may not know exactly what it is they're feeling or where it's coming from, but it will arrive. In that way, you write the definition of every relationship you have, and no connection ever has to end unless you choose for it to. By keeping it alive, you strengthen their story, and you strengthen your own.

"Close your eyes, Ophelia. See each of those people in front of you, one at a time. Feel the love you have for each of them. Let it surface. Then send it in a line of light from who you are to who they are. Keep sending it until you feel complete."

I really liked the idea, but it also made me nervous, though I didn't know why. I closed my eyes and did as Gusto suggested. The first person came to mind, and I felt the love I had for them... let it fill me... surface... then imagined it going from me to them... a wave of light... they were there... there was the love, the light...

I quickly opened my eyes and said, "It's not working."

He knew me well enough to sense the panic in my voice but didn't seem worried. In fact, he seemed to be trying to hide a smile. "What's not working?" he said.

"The more I allow myself to really feel the love inside me, the more it seems to consume me. I'm sending it, but I feel like it's still there in me—*building* actually... I feel almost dizzy. The love is... it's overwhelming."

"You're not releasing it, my Ophelia. You're not giving it away. You're offering it and holding on to it at the same time. You're worried about how they'll respond to it—and whether or not they'll respond at all. You're wondering whether it will come back to you."

He was right. I knew it because my stomach stopped turning in circles, and a calmness came over me.

"Feel that love and share it. And then—let go. Always let go when you love, my Ophelia. Love and let go."

I closed my eyes and pictured the line of light going from the core of me to the core of the first person in my heart and on my mind…

Love through light…

The light of love…

I kept doing it—over and over—until, when it arrived at the person, I was finally able to let go of it, simply giving it to them to do with it whatever they chose.

Then I moved on to the next person… and the next…

* * *

When I felt complete, I opened my eyes.

"Thank you," Gusto said.

Of course he was one of the many I sent love to.

Turning my attention to the starfish in my hand, I said, "I'm going to take this with me as a reminder."

"Yes. Good idea."

As I put the starfish in my pocket, Gusto shook his head. "That's not necessary."

"But you just said it was a good idea…"

"Yes!" He pointed to my pocket. "But not there!" He held his hand over his heart and said, "Here, Ophelia. *Here.* You're still connected. As long as you choose to be."

I took the starfish out of my pocket and placed it back in the sand. I started tracing in the sand around each of its arms, down the V between, around the tip of the arm, down and then up the next V, continuing until I looked up and noticed Gusto, sitting so still. His hand had remained on his heart. He seemed both present and elsewhere, gazing into my eyes.

His hand, his heart...

It sent shivers through me and cradled my spirit. Something was happening in that moment. Not there with us, not there on the island. Yet I was on the receiving end. It was coming to me from all different directions. I sat there, taking it all in, unable to pull my eyes from his hand over his heart.

A girl in my sixth-grade class. She was new to the school, from Scotland, though it wasn't her accent that made her stand out. It was her clothes. Her frizzy, mousy brown, un-styled hair. Her black, clunky shoes. One day at recess, when no one else could hear me, I told her I liked her socks—knee socks. The rest of us wore ankle socks. Now. With her daughter, comforting her, telling the story of how a friendship began. A promise to her daughter: she was never alone. It was coming to me from her: *Love through light. The light of love.*

The kind, old man who worked at the grocery store I frequented. He had a different greeting for each day of the week. Monday, it was "Milady! How lovely to see you!" Tuesday, it was "Knock-knock." He hadn't seen me in a while. It was coming to me from him: *Love through light. The light of love.*

My sister. I hadn't spoken to her in some time. She was thinking about how when we were little, when things were simpler, we used to play house together with our Pillsbury Doughboy dolls. It was coming to me from her: *Love through light. The light of love.*

A flickering of a moment. A single thought about me. *Love through light. The light of love.*

And then much more than a single thought. A melody of vibrations, the notes of an oboe, drifting, catching on a branch, falling with a leaf, rising on the wind, becoming the air itself. Its music filled me, consumed me, held me. From my husband to me…

Love through light. The light of love.

The strings of a violin joining in. Reaching higher, trembling with joy. From my daughter to me…

Love through light. The light of love.

In that moment, I experienced and understood the ultimate purpose of connectedness.

Gusto hugged me and then walked off without a word, an extra skip in his step.

I took off my flip-flop and wrote while humming a song that came from the deepest part of me.

Love and let go. Freely. Generously.

Allow people to be who they are, noticing those
rhythms that are harmonized with mine, sometimes a
drumbeat, sometimes the whistle of a flute, bringing out
music that wouldn't otherwise exist, and then eventually,
there will be no one in my life who doesn't in some way
or another encourage me to sing.

I trust myself to remember who I am.
Always. I have it in me.

27. The Volume of Others

I received a letter back from the bride.

Never contact me or my ex-husband again, the first line said. They were divorced now. Four months into their marriage.

I knew there was something off about you from the moment I met you, she went on to say. *I don't know why I let my ex convince me you two were the right photographers for us. I should have been more adamant than he was, because I could see what you were like. I've known people like you. Angry, a mean streak, jealous. That was it, wasn't it? Being in a tired marriage like yours, you couldn't stand to see two people happy. Of course! Your husband starts looking at you differently. Looking elsewhere. That's what happened, isn't it? He was looking, wasn't he? I bet it was more than just looking. And I bet it wasn't the first time. I feel sorry for you, not because you don't deserve that, but because you think an apology can fix what you've done. You're out of your mind.*

What if someone had done it to you? Have you done this to other people? Do you have a daughter? If so, I hope she gets you out of her life before you ruin hers.

The letter was three pages long, the last lines spilling over onto the final page: *It was about time you put it in writing—what you did. You have no idea of the hell I've been through for the last four months of my life because of you. You maliciously planted seeds of doubt by leaving us out of every picture.*

She finished by saying her lawyer now, no longer theirs, would be in touch with us again. More damages would be collected now that divorce was added to the list of emotional and mental injuries suffered.

I knew then that what was left in savings, just enough to cover our daughter's tuition, was as good as gone.

I left only the last page of the letter on my husband's desk in his office. I burned the rest of the pages. I had already subjected him to enough. He didn't deserve to be pulled down into a pit of lies along with everything else.

My daughter. That's all I could see then. Her voice was all I could hear. I had no idea how to tell her what I had to take away from her.

28. The Must

It was late afternoon when I arrived. Gusto was whistling away, pulling a boat down to the water's edge.

He saw me and said, "Welcome back, my friend!"

I was mesmerized by the rustic beauty of the boat. It was a potpourri of wood Gusto found in the jungle. I remembered the day I saw him cutting bamboo and realized he had been working on the boat for some time now. I wondered if he had been up all night and worked straight through the day. He kind of looked like it.

He handed me the oars and then dragged the boat into the water and stepped into it. "Ready?"

Saying no didn't feel right, so I gave him a tentative yes.

Gusto did a little celebration dance, started to lose his balance, and almost fell over the side of the boat. "Let's go then!"

He put his hand out, took the oars, and helped me in the boat.

We sat down, and Gusto started rowing us away from the shore, humming as he did so. After a few minutes, he looked at me and said, "You won't make a song with me? What's the matter?"

I was wondering how well the makeshift boat would keep us afloat, but I knew that's not what Gusto was really asking me. I thought of saying that I was fine, that nothing was wrong, but if I had a mango for every time Gusto told me how important honesty was and how it brought me back to life, he'd never have to look for another mango. Ever.

I told him the truth. "I'm nervous about having no idea how anything will turn out."

"Why?" He seemed genuinely confused.

"I've just never taken the kind of chances I'm about to. I can't help but think, what if I'm wrong?"

"If you're wrong? I don't understand. If I think I'm picking a mango, but it turns out to be a guava, what's the problem? I still eat! Maybe I didn't sleep enough."

With that, he handed me the oars and took a much-deserved nap.

With a tightness in my throat, I watched the island grow smaller as I rowed us farther away.

* * *

Gusto almost tipped the boat again when he woke up. He jumped up and immediately announced, "I just had the most beautiful dreams! I never dreamed anything like it! A moss-covered moon, mountains of mangos, masts decorated with marbles, a mirror that melted into a mirage, mint and melon and mist… it was magnificent! How about you? Did you sleep?"

I shook my head.

Gusto pointed at me. "You have a secret… Ah-ha! Did you dream?"

"In a way."

"Yes! What did you dream about?"

"My life."

"And?"

"Magical moments."

"Yes! That's the spirit! We need music!"

Gusto started whistling and took one of the oars. We took turns rowing—Gusto, then me, Gusto, then me. When our arms grew tired, we leaned back and looked up at the evening sky, letting the boat just drift.

After a few minutes, he said. "You want magic. Yes?"

"Definitely."

"Then you have to be okay with maybes, and there's a must."

"What's the must?"

"Trust. If you want magic, you can't know how the pieces will come together until they do. You don't *want* to know everything ahead of time. And this too, my Ophelia: if you try so hard to figure it all out, you might end up saying, 'No! Not a chance! Absolutely not!' to real possibilities—because you're basing all the 'possible' hows and whos and wheres on what you've experienced in your life up to that point. And so then... the must is *trust*. Trust what you don't know."

I thought about it. "It sounds so simple—to trust—but I don't always know how to do that."

"How do you find a cave in the jungle? Focus on what you *do* know. You know what you want. And I know I'm hungry." Gusto reached into his pocket and pulled out two guavas. He took his knife, sliced the guavas open, and handed one to me.

"When the want for change knocks on your door, it doesn't work to pretend you don't hear it. It will only knock louder. And that's a very good thing. Change pushes you forward, takes you by the hand, and leads you to more of who you are. Look at all those stars starting to come out in the sky. Which one is pulling you toward it? Reach for it. Don't put it off because you don't know how to get there or what it will look like when you do. Be fearless and adventurous! It's your life sitting before you, and you have the opportunity to do with it what you want.

"When you hear the knocking at your door—Tap! Tap!—celebrate. It's a good thing that change is even possible. Imagine if it were not!"

Every time he said the word *change,* there was such a finality to it, like a shift had already taken place. Something was knocking at the door, many things actually, but I felt like Gusto had already opened the door and invited it all in. Suddenly I realized why. I sat up and looked around us. Then I looked again. *"Gusto."*

"Yes."

"Where's our island?"

"It's where it's always been."

 I felt sick to my stomach. "I don't like this."

"I didn't do this—not alone. Sometimes you make a quiet decision and give permission to your Gusto to take over, to lead the way. That's also when you invite the magic in."

"But you—" I stopped. "I don't know if I can do this."

"You can. Breathe…"

 I took a deep breath and then probably ten more. Slowly, I surrendered to all the uncertainty surrounding me. I surrendered to not knowing where I was. I surrendered to not knowing where I was going. I surrendered to not understanding the ocean. Another deep breath. I surrendered to the tides having a say of their own. I surrendered to the fear that we might have left our island for good. Another deep breath. I surrendered to the sadness about the magical moments—that I could only remember them from the past, not confidently see them in the future. With the next breath, long and deep, I realized that even though I was scared, I felt safe. "Okay," I said.

"Well done, my Ophelia. Well done. Change can be scary. Maybe sometimes it's heartbreaking or confusing. Maybe it means having to first say goodbye. There's always someone, something, or a place you're letting go of when you make a change in your life—even when you're leaving something you're ready to leave. But when it's right, it's right. Even if it doesn't make sense yet." He gestured to the ocean surrounding us. "Even if you don't know how you're possibly going to get to where you want to go. Because here's the matter of it: if you focus on how you want to feel, it will work out. You'll get there.

"Dance confidently into the unknowns. You don't always need to have all the guavas in place first. This is when anything is possible! Can you feel the excitement? We can go north, south, east, west! Anywhere in between."

I felt it. A nervous excitement.

"Ha-ha!" Gusto pointed to a star shooting across the sky, chasing after who knows what. "Yes," he said. "While change may be unsettling, what's far more so is not making a change when you know it's time. Answer the door and see who or what's knocking; it's never as scary as you think it will be. Then ride your wave. Climb to your star. Grab life by the reins and chart your course. *This is your life!*"

"That's what I don't understand," I said. "Am I supposed to just go with the flow or am I supposed to make things happen? How can I ride the wave and chart my course at the same time?"

155

"Excellent question! ...I don't know."

"Are you kidding?"

"Yes, of course! This is how. Feel your way. Chart your course by giving your attention to the end result, the destination, how you want to feel. See the shore in front of you, no matter where you are. And then along the way, follow your instincts. Paddle into and ride the waves that call to you, without judging them as too big or too little, without worrying about where they'll take you or how riding this wave or that wave is connected to the end result. Some waves will take more effort; you'll paddle with strength and determination. Others will lift you up with your first effort at becoming one with them. One wave after another. No judging. Only feeling and then doing. Enjoy the ride, Ophelia. Oh, yes... enjoy it with all you heart, all your being. Thank it. Love it."

"I like that a lot. And it helps." I picked up the oars; it felt like we had been drifting too long, and it was time... for something. But I couldn't make myself row. They felt so heavy and uncooperative in my hands. I put them back down. "I think I know what the problem is. It's that I try to believe in something higher, a bigger force at work, but sometimes I wonder if that's naïve or wishful thinking. I don't know for sure that there are any forces at work other than our own.

"Before going to the island, I kept finding myself in this place where I'd try to get really quiet and listen for an answer, some guidance. I thought of going to a church—any church. I hadn't been to one in so long, but I felt drawn just to sit there where the possibility of something greater exists. I hoped to hear something, a voice talking to me. I guess I wanted an epiphany."

"Yes," Gusto said. "It's like the radio. If there's nothing being said or sung at the station itself, you'll hear only static or silence when you tune in. You *are* the station; *you're* the source. The guidance has to come from you first. What do you hear inside you? That you're on track or that you're not? That you're in tune or out of tune? All outside guidance only confirms what you already know— but you won't hear it clearly, or sometimes at all, unless you're first willing to know what you already know. You see, Ophelia, you need to *trust* what *you* know."

"It keeps coming back to trust."

"Yes, it does. It's a decision. To trust yourself. To trust your life. To trust the uncertainties."

I picked up the oars again but still couldn't get myself to start rowing. I felt paralyzed in the darkness, my hands gripping them but not moving. I started to wonder if we'd just drift there forever. It didn't feel right to do that, but I didn't know how to move us away from the place of uncertainty I was in.

"Ophelia, you *know* who you are. You *know* who and what you trust in. *Be Ophelia.* Be strong. Accept no limitations. Put no constraints on what's possible. Let the magic begin. You know how to open the door wide and let the magic all the way in. You know well. *Trust.* Even when things look ugly and you're sitting in an uncomfortable position. Even when you don't know which direction you're going or which way to turn. You *know* you're wise. You *know* your instincts are trustworthy. You *know* the answers will come. You *know* you'll hear them. You *know* you're not alone, that there *are* forces at work that you can't see. You *know* that life is beautiful, that sometimes it's bitter, sometimes sweet, but that every drop of it is delectable. Oh, what a word! My friend, you *know* that not only do things work out for the best, they work out better than you could possibly imagine. Even when you don't see it or feel it, when there's no reason to believe it, you *know* it. You know it because you decide to know it. And then it is so."

I looked around, and as obvious as it was, I realized that the ocean had no signs and no roads, so in a way, the darkness we were cloaked in didn't even matter. I could row, or we could drift. I could trust myself and my life— or not. It didn't take more than a split second to hear which choice the voice inside was begging me to make.

In the moment I made that choice, I made another— to move into and through the uncertainties instead of trying to move away from them. I felt myself becoming the gentle waves surrounding us, leaping, reaching, touching something invisible. As I became the water, I felt no boundaries and no limitations. Only freedom and possibility. I stopped seeing what I was about to do as risky or scary and started to feel like I was about to really live my life.

Gusto leaned back, put his arms behind his head, and stared up at the sky, a huge smile on his face. "Believe in magic because that unseen force you wonder about, that you *trust* in, is the magic of love. You are love. And you're surrounded by it."

He looked like he was going to say something else but seemed to be hesitating.

"What is it?" I asked.

"My proudest moment is when I get to sit back and watch you navigating with just one compass: total and complete trust. In yourself. In your life."

I looked down. I had started rowing—without thinking about it. I had no idea which direction I was taking us in, but the act of rowing resonated with every part of me. There was a rhythm to it. It wasn't forced. I was surrendering to a thousand unknowns and deliberately moving forward at the same time. Being the captain made me feel wildly alive.

Not wanting to let go of the oars, I made a mental note of what to write on my flip-flop:

When in the midst of making a change,
there's excitement in the unknowns and uncertainties.
I trust myself.
I trust my life.

29. The Volume of Now

I picked up the phone and then put it back down, paced around the room, picked it up again and dialed.

My daughter answered. It had been a long time since we'd spoken. Without the enthusiasm that used to carry her voice, she caught me up on school and her friends and then said, "I don't think it's what you called to talk about."

"Honey…" I choked back the tears, my throat tight. "We're going to have to figure out a different school for you next year… or… other options."

She started crying. "I know. Dad told me."

"I'm so sorry. I'm so, so sorry. I'll figure out how to make more money. I'll figure out a way to—"

"No… it's not that."

We both waited until she composed herself enough to keep talking. I was glad she couldn't see me, my nails digging into my palm.

"What about you and Dad?" she said. "Are you going to make it?"

I took a deep breath. "I don't know."

"No, Mom. Don't say that. Don't say you don't know. This can all fall apart, everything. All of it, including school. But our family can't."

"I just don't feel like I can make any promises. I don't want to lie to you."

"I'm not going to lie to you either. You're the one who called me, so I hope you're ready to hear what I have to say. I know you're not happy and that you haven't been for a long time. And Dad too. But I also know that I've never seen two people more in love. It used to embarrass me how you and Dad held hands everywhere we went. I saw the way you two looked at each other and teased each other, constantly touching, and I thought, *They're acting like teenagers. Even I don't act like that.* Do you remember when I went through that phase sophomore year of never wanting to be home? I spent more and more time at different friends' houses, and their parents were around sometimes, and I saw them, what was normal for other people, and that's when I realized how lucky I was."

She was quiet for a moment. "I know you two aren't happy, but never once—not for a minute—have I believed it has anything to do with you choosing to spend your life with Dad, or him deciding to spend his with you. It's that you two haven't been on the same page for a long time. But the thing is, Mom, neither of you has liked that separate page you're on. It's so lonely watching you two being lonely. And it's frustrating because I know that as soon as you two decide to get on a new page—*together*—everything will be fine. Way more than fine, actually." She exhaled. "I didn't realize I had so much to say."

I could barely breathe, let alone speak, I was crying so hard. I closed my eyes for a moment, trying to focus, willing myself to get my emotions under control. "I love you," I said, my voice cracking. "And I'm… I'm so sorry."

"I know you are. And I love you too."

I took a few deep breaths. "I'm not sure what happens next, but I'll think about everything you said."

"Okay."

"I'm going to go now."

I waited for her to say goodbye, but instead she said, "Wait. Remember what you used to say to me? When I was five and lost my favorite blanket at that hotel we stayed at? The maids had accidentally taken it with the sheets, and it was so torn from me taking it everywhere I went, it probably got thrown away somewhere in the laundry room of the hotel. I cried and cried and wouldn't eat or talk, and then after I don't even know how much time passed, you sat me down and said, 'You don't need to be sad anymore. It's okay to be happy again.' I was looking at my toys when you said that. I hadn't touched them all day, and all I wanted to do was play, but I felt like I couldn't, that I shouldn't. So I asked if you were sure, and you said yes, and I asked you how you knew for sure, and you smiled and looked out past the balcony of the hotel room. 'I can hear it,' you said. 'A voice is telling me it's time for fun again.' And then you looked at me and said, 'Go ahead. Play. It's okay.' I can still see the look in your eyes when you said that. It made me believe you. And then the first time my heart broke, when that boy whose name I don't even remember decided he didn't want to be my boyfriend after only one week. And probably a hundred other times, you let me cry and be sad, and then eventually you'd say to me, 'You don't have to suffer anymore.' I know you remember this one—when you left your journal on the counter, you and I were in a fight, and I read it, knowing it was the most hurtful thing I could do to you. When you saw me with it open in front of me, you cried so hard, Mom. I knew I had done something I would always regret. I couldn't forgive myself. And then you—the one I purposely hurt—you're the one who sat me down, gave me a hug, and said, 'It's time for the suffering to end.'" She was silent for a moment, and then she said, "Mom... the suffering needs to end. *Now. It's time.*"

30. The Matter of Specifics

Sometime while rowing, I had fallen asleep, and when I woke up, it was from an unsettled, restless sleep, though I couldn't pinpoint why. I got up, looked around, and was surprised there was still no shore in sight.

Gusto didn't seem to be bothered at all. He didn't seem to notice that it was overcast and looked like a downpour was minutes away. In fact, he seemed to be thoroughly enjoying it. He had his legs draped over the side of the boat with his feet in the water. The oars were sitting on the bottom of the boat, and he seemed content to just lie there, rocking back and forth—though the motion of the boat was far from gentle.

"Do you want me to row again?" I said. "Shouldn't we head somewhere?"

He thought for a minute and then said, "Maybe. But you've had quite the night. No rowing for now. Come sit next to me. You don't look steady standing there."

I lay down next to him and put my feet in the water next to his.

"So then. Much better."

As we lay there side by side, I thought about what had kept me up a lot of the night while I rowed us into the unknowns. Where would I live when I went back? Where we lived before, or would we move? Together? Could I find a place that made me feel as vivid and alive and in tune with who I was as the island did? Did a place like that even exist in "real life"? What would I do for a job? Photography, or would I switch tracks, follow a different passion? Could I afford to? That just brought up more questions and unknowns because it wasn't just about me. There were other people to consider. There always are, I realized. And then there were the things I wasn't sure Gusto could really understand, things like logistics and commitments and—

"Have you noticed that the only time you wonder if I 'can really understand' is when you're in your mind? You want me to go there with you. But I won't. You know that, too. That's not who Gusto is. I'm content understanding that you're in your mind, and I'm not. I live in your heart. But want to know a secret? When two people are both in their heart instead of their head, they always understand each other. Always."

I knew he was right. It was starting to be almost ridiculously obvious when I was in my head as opposed to my heart. But still... that's where I was, so I told him what was bothering me. "What if when I go back, my life doesn't look *anything* like I want it to—if my vision is completely different from my reality? I'm pretty sure it will be… unless I have total amnesia."

He smiled. "No. You remember well. Rather than looking back over your shoulder though, look forward. Focus on your vision. Believe in it and give it your attention. Some people say, 'Before I knew it, it happened.' But I say, once you know it, it will happen. If you focus on what you want and know it in your heart to *be*—to in some way exist already—that becomes your reality."

"What if I'm not positive about what I want or where I want to live or what I want to do?"

"No problem! Don't be afraid to experiment with ideas, try out different paths. Sometimes a kiwi. Sometimes a banana. Peel it back. Taste it. Each one will create a richer you. You don't have to be so very sure. Simply tap into who you are and then let that point the way to everything else. Feel your way. One step at a time. If you don't like fruit salad, why try to decide which fruits would go together? Why not just eat them alone, one at a time?"

Gusto lay back and laughed.

"My Ophelia, I have some advice for you. Are you listening?"

"Of course."

"Do what makes you happy."

My first reaction was to think that it was simple advice—too simple. I pictured me doing whatever I wanted to do all day long.

"But wouldn't that make me totally irresponsible—to just do what I wanted to? Or what if it hurt someone—me just doing what I wanted to. I don't think it's a realistic way to live, and more than that…"

He was smiling, watching me.

I was about to say, "…it wouldn't make me happy." But I stopped myself because it hit me that Gusto had said *Do what makes you happy,* not *Do whatever you want to.* Acting irresponsibly wouldn't make me happy. Nor would hurting someone. That I knew.

He said, "Do you see?"

"I think so."

"Do what makes you happy…

"Feel the feelings that make you happy. The ones that make you excited to jump out of bed when the sun peeks into the morning sky. The ones that give you butterflies during the middle of an ordinary day. The ones that leave you smiling when your head's on your pillow and you're about to give yourself over to the night and dreams and all that happens within you while you sleep.

"Think the thoughts that make you happy. First thing when you wake up, all through your day, and the last thoughts you think before you go to sleep. Choose thoughts that make you happy. Say things to yourself that make you smile. It may not always be the first thought that comes into your mind. Or even the second or third. But you'll know when you've found the thoughts that make you happy because they'll immediately carry you right to the peak of any mountain you're trying to climb. Every time.

"Do the things that make you happy. In each minute. Each day. There's a way. Yes. You may not see it immediately, but if you intend to do what makes you happy, that's everything you'll do—no matter what you're doing. Do what you love doing. It's your destiny, Ophelia. What makes you the happiest, that's your destiny, to do what only you can do—because there is no other like you.

"Surround yourself with people who make you happy, the people whose song lifts your own to what it could not otherwise be. Thank them. Love them.

"Live in a space that makes you happy, one where you know you belong. A space that warms your soul with a gentle wind that feeds your spark until it becomes a flame… and then keeps it there.

"All of it. Not just one of those. *All of it.* You're meant to know happiness. Do you know that?"

"Yes."

"Really?"

"I do."

"Okay then. Remember we talked about the matter of intending? Intend happiness, knowing it's in no way single or limited. And then—Plop! Plop! The pieces will fall into place around you. And it will happen with a texture so much more magnificent than perfection. Don't look for them to fall into place perfectly; look for the raw beauty."

"I like that a lot."

"Me, too," he said.

"What about money, though?"

"What about it?"

"It's always such a deciding factor."

"Then it will be."

I smiled. "I knew you'd say that."

"Of course! If you let it, it will be. You already know what happens when you decide to believe money takes a long time to grow, that there sometimes isn't enough. Yes? Then money takes a long time to grow, and there sometimes isn't enough. You know already what happens when you decide to believe you should make decisions based on money alone. Money becomes the matter of it all. Your life runs in circles around it. Does that work for you? Does that make you happy? If I taste a persimmon and don't like it—maybe that wouldn't happen, but anyway— should I keep eating it, forcing myself to swallow the bad taste? Did I keep eating rollinias? No! I am Gusto!

"It's the same with beliefs, Ophelia. If you don't like the results, try something different.

"If you think, *There's not enough time,* there won't be. If you believe you have plenty of time, you will. Something will cancel itself out. Time will *open up;* it will create itself to match your belief. Awhile back, you said things manifest much faster on the island than in your life. You *believe* that, and so you see and experience that. Do you see? Time is yours to bend and shape as you choose. It's incredible, really! If you say, 'I'm too busy. I don't have time to do what makes me happy,' then of course—it's simple!—you won't find yourself with time to do what makes you happy. And if you decide, 'I can do what I want to do *today*, right now,' time will shape itself accordingly. If you believe, *This is going to take a long time, too long,* have no doubt—it will. And if you say, 'This is going to go smoothly and quickly'—*presto!* Your belief is your command. You are in charge, Ophelia! It's always the same!

"If you think you have few choices, you'll have few choices. If you believe the possibilities are endless, they will be. If you think there's no way something can work out, of course it won't. If you say, 'I don't know how to do this yet, but at some point I will,' at some point you most certainly will. Just like ease. If you think things will happen with ease, they will. If you believe they'll be difficult, that's exactly what you'll experience. Why do you think you're here with me? *Because you believe it's possible!*

"It's no different with money. You can let it be the driver or you can take the driver's seat and believe that plenty of money will come along for the ride, no matter where you go."

"But what if I actually don't have enough, and it's stopping me from doing some of the things I want to do?"

"Focus on what you *do* have and what you're able to create today. I think you'll be surprised. Unless, of course… Do you want to keep believing that you don't have enough? That something like money is actually more powerful than you are? You can point at money or time or circumstance or a forest of other things. But then you're pretending you're not in charge—throwing the key out and climbing into the trunk of the car. No more of that. You take the wheel. All the specifics and all that you need will come along for the ride; you're the driver to your destiny.

"Aren't you curious? Don't you wonder what might happen if you do what makes you happy and believe all the pieces will fall into place? Even money?" He looked at me and winked. "I already know what would happen. So do you. The question is… are you ready for it?"

The rain started coming down, first in drizzles, and then fast, heavy drops. Gusto closed his eyes and smiled. "Do what makes you happy, Ophelia." With that, he closed his eyes and somehow fell asleep as the rain soaked him.

I sat thinking for a while. I hadn't said much toward the end, and I wondered if he noticed. I wanted to stop worrying about money and time and the rest of the specifics, but I also wanted to be honest with myself. I couldn't just change those beliefs like the flip of a switch.

I *wanted* to. I wanted so badly to be able to, because it felt like the last and final step, but something was stopping me. I couldn't do it without pretending I believed something I didn't actually believe.

That bottom-line belief—I couldn't put it into words. All I knew was that it felt like a faulty circuit breaker that kept flipping certain switches back down every time I tried to flick them up. Hard as I tried, I couldn't figure out what that master belief was.

I thought that maybe if I looked at some of the notes I had written, it would give me some clarity; something Gusto had said in the past might trigger a new awareness.

That's when it hit me.

I shook him awake. "Gusto! We have to go back. *Now.*" A knot twisted in my stomach.

"We *are* going back," he said, his voice groggy.

"No—to the island. I'm serious, Gusto—we have to go back now. I forgot my flip-flops. I wrote down everything. I won't be able to remember it…"

He was already asleep.

"Gusto… please…"

I knew in that moment I was on my own.

31. The Departure Call

After hanging up with my daughter, I couldn't get those words out of my head. *The suffering needs to end. Now. It's time.*

Did she mean her suffering?

Her father's?

It made me dizzy, trying to figure out whose suffering needed to end. How to end it.

And that island. I barely remembered that voice, let alone mentioning it to her.

I went for a walk to clear my head, having no idea where I was heading.

With my thoughts swirling, ping-ponging around my head, suffocating my heart, I returned home with tulips. I reached into the top cabinet above the kitchen sink, pulled out the nearest vase, and wiped the dust off with a paper towel.

32. The Storm

Hours later, still awake, I knelt and looked over the side of the boat, peering into the darkness of the ocean, not sure what I was looking for, not sure what I might see—a tiny hope that my flip-flops might suddenly float up, the words intact. The deeper I looked for them, the more the water seemed to be rising up, reaching toward me, surrounding me, becoming a mirage between me and what I was trying to see.

And then I saw it—a vision. Me kneeling, surrounded by broken glass. Each piece of reflective glass on the floor was talking to me about choices I had made in the past, experiences that, through my own doing, had brought me to my knees. I tried to make myself stand up in my vision, but the water on the ground was so slippery, and each piece of glass pulled at me, speaking of a past thought associated with a past experience: *You're too… and you're too… and too… You're too…*

On and on they went. I couldn't silence them. I couldn't make myself stand up, move far enough away from the broken pieces to get perspective. I couldn't make the leap from on my knees, to on the island, to in the boat, to back on my knees... and standing up.

The sharp thoughts pierced my core, my essence, my peace... but at the same time, there was something comforting about their familiarity. I understood them. And the more I thought about it, the idea of letting those words go terrified me. What would I do without them?

It felt like jumping into a void, and I had no idea where I would land. In a paradise of mangos, palm trees, sad and happy hats, sharing snakes, a pair of flip-flops that became my canvas, rocks that spoke to me, pelicans that carried me, a tree house of my own... how realistic was that? How long could any of those feelings and beliefs really last back in the real world? At least, I told myself, I knew I was grounded in reality. I told myself I wasn't giving into fear; I was just learning to be happy with the way things were.

Even more than that, I was starting to think I couldn't live up to Gusto's expectations. I had made so many mistakes. My faults were real. My weaknesses still a part of me. And in reality, I didn't live in a perfect world on a tropical island.

I pulled myself back from the vision I seemed to have become a part of. It was time to say goodbye to Gusto. I turned to wake him and tell him, and that's when I realized I was in the water. And that Gusto wasn't there. And neither was the boat.

* * *

The swell was rising. Three feet. Five feet. Seven. I was rising and crashing with it, unable to see much through the pelting rain and the waves closing in on me. The wind was relentless, circling so quickly, building momentum. I felt it pulling itself together and then pushing me down.

The sky was getting darker and heavier. I started treading water as fast as I could, trying not to think about the weight of the waves curling over on me, pushing me under, holding me there… "Gusto!"

The rain came down harder, and I saw lightning in the distance. Then I heard the thunder. I started counting. *One, two, three, four, five, six*—lightning again.

"Gusto!"

I turned in so many circles, sure he was right there— no, right there—over that crest—but the crest kept rising. I couldn't see him anywhere.

My mind was racing.

"What am I doing wrong?" I yelled.

No answer.

"What's happening?"

Thunder preceded lightning. Four seconds between.

"Gusto! Where are you?"

* * *

Hours went by. I was exhausted. I couldn't fight it anymore. *You're too...* My mind came up with nonstop endings, and every time I heard one of those thoughts, I lost more energy, felt the weight of the dark depth pull me closer to it. Finally, I reached the point where I gave into the thoughts. In that moment, I hated myself—that was the truth of it. I was disappointed in myself; I was a joke, and I knew it. All that time and effort on the island. What a waste. Had I really thought it could last?

I stopped treading, closed my eyes, and let myself start sinking. The darkness of the deep enveloped me, and I realized how easy it was just to let myself give in and fall away. Down. Deeper.

The flame inside me was getting smaller and smaller. I felt so thick and muddy... and ugly. I couldn't believe that at one time I thought myself to be beautiful. Or deserving of anything better in any way.

Or deserving of anything better in any way.

It was in that moment, when that thought went through me, that I couldn't ignore the wildness of my heartbeat.

Urging me to hear it.

I chose to. For no reason other than wanting to know what someone's heart says to them when it's already said all there is to say.

Lightning racing down into the black water in front of me, a mirage—I could see a spark. And then the words I had expressed, they came back.

My heart spoke clearly. Not in a whisper, but in a voice that overpowered all others within me.

I create. I choose.

The spark in front of me, cradled by the black water, grew larger, began swaying.

I'm the architect of my life. I'm the builder. I have all the tools I need.

I have dreams. I remember. I reach for the star that calls to me. I'm my own star.

I'm limitless.

I'm life.

I am Ophelia.

The flame in front of me—orange now, its tips blue—alive beneath the water, reaching out toward me. Dancing. Holding its hands out to me. Urging. Asking for even more.

My heart continued speaking to me.

I make mistakes. I exceed expectations. I have days filled with color. I have gray moments. I have doubts. I believe. I'm not perfect. I'm exactly who I want to be. I recognize what fulfills me. I know when something drains me. I try. I fall. I stand up.

The flame, wild with delight, twirling around me, creating a barrier between me and the dense, black water.

My heart went on.

I'm fearless. Sometimes I let myself forget that and am afraid. I'm a healer. Sometimes I let myself forget that and cause hurt. I'm brave. Sometimes I let myself forget that and am shy with the world when it's best not to be. I'm generous. Sometimes I let myself forget that and pull into myself. I forgive myself. I forgive others. Sometimes I let myself forget that and am angry. I am light. Sometimes I let myself forget that and have trouble seeing through the darkness. I'm grateful. Sometimes I let myself forget that and feel smaller than I am. I'm happy. Sometimes I let myself forget that and am sad.

The flame and I joined, becoming one.

I won't give up. I won't let it go out.

I focused on rising up through the water, breaking through the surface so I could breathe again. With that intention, I felt the breath of trust inside me. A surge of hope quickly followed.

I'm good.

The words pushing me up.

I'm enough.

Higher and higher.

I believe in me.

A giant push upward.

And then—the master circuit breaker:

I am worthy.

The last push propelled me to the surface. I broke through the water and immediately sucked in a huge breath of air, pulling the wildly passionate flame of life all the way inside me.

I am worthy.

Click. Click.

I am worthy.

Switch after switch flipped. Quickly. Easily.

I am worthy.

The water wasn't pulling me down; it was buoying me. The wind blew the rain far away from me. The clouds parted and allowed the dawning sun to shine. I could see. And in that moment, I had not a single doubt that I was supported in every way.

I am worthy.

That's when I saw Gusto. And our boat.

Gusto was leaning over the side, reaching for me. He pulled me into the boat and wrapped a blanket around me. I curled up and rested my head on Gusto's lap. He gently stroked my hair, pulling the wet strands away from my face.

"Do you understand what's happening, Ophelia?"

"I think so."

"Come out of the storm *for good*. Let the sun in. Let it wrap itself around you. Take in its rays and let them move through and around you. Listen to the ocean. To the waves, ebbing, flowing. Back and forth. Calmly now. When you're ready to fly, which you will be—I can promise you—stand up, open your arms wide, take a deep breath. Breathe in your life. Release. Then lift your face to the sun, speak to it with your eyes, and get ready to fly."

Gusto started humming softly, and I drifted into a deep sleep.

* * *

I dreamed that we were back on our island, eating mangos on the beach. So many mangos. I got down to the pit of the first one and suddenly remembered that terrifying night in the water. I said, "When I'm not here with you, it feels like I'm in a place between two trapezes. I need to know what to do with myself there. Where were you, Gusto? When I was in the water? Where were you?"

He took my hands in his, looked me in the eye, and told me what I already knew. Of course he was there.

"I'm sorry," I said.

"Why?"

"You looked so sad when you pulled me into the boat."

"Of course. Because you were losing me. And I was losing you. I don't think you understand how that happens."

"I do. It's when I'm angry. Or when I'm scared. That's when I've felt it happen in the past."

Gusto slowly shook his head.

"No?"

"No. It's not when you feel angry or sad or disappointed or frustrated or scared. Feel however you feel! No matter the feeling.

"It's when you think perfection is a must for living with gusto. Trust is the only must. Remember? When you think perfection is the must, you decide you're unworthy. Of more. Or better. *No.*

"You are worthy. Always. End of sentence. *Because you don't have to be perfect to be worthy.*

"Your mind is a tool, an important one. It creates the thoughts you think. But those thoughts have to resonate with your *heart,* to wildly fan the flame inside you. If they don't, they hold you under who you are. It was when you moved into your heart and you heard and felt the truth of who you are that you began to rise from the heavy darkness, up to where I was waiting for you.

"You see, when you don't first support yourself with the core belief of *I'm worthy,* you won't feel the support of any of the external, outside-of-yourself specifics in your life—people, places, circumstances, time, money, and more. But when you flip that master switch, every kind of support that ever existed—and new ones too—they show up readily, easily, practically fighting to be first in line.

"I don't fade because of any feeling you feel. I fade when you think of me as someone separate from you, when you forget who you really are.

"But you remembered. Yes, Ophelia. You chose to remember.

"Hold on to it. Cradle it. Especially when you make mistakes, when you see something and you think you have a reason not to like yourself. And when you're embarrassed or sorry or wish you could turn back time. Do you want to know why? I'll tell you. Because if you hold on to who you really are, you'll always love yourself—even in those moments. You'll know that you're worthy of every happiness you've ever dreamed of. Always.

"You see, there will be times when you know exactly what to say, when the words that come out feel oh so inspired! And there will be moments when you wish you had it in you to say anything, when you wish you could say things better. No matter of it. Just be honest with yourself. There will be times when you feel like the sun, and there will be moments when you feel like the clouds that hide the sun. You'll make choices that leave a sweet taste in your mouth, and you'll make choices that leave a sour taste. You'll be at your best at times, like the mango when it's perfectly ripe. And you'll have moments when you think you couldn't possibly go lower, a mango that has fallen, bruising itself as it landed. Don't worry. These are only seasons, my friend. It's only the matter of being honest with yourself. I'll tell you why.

"When you're honest, that's when you taste freedom. That's when anything is possible and there are no limits. Because honesty rearranges the space.

"Be a pirate and search for treasures if that's part of who you are. Stand up and clap if that's who you are. Sit in a rocking chair and watch every sunset if that's who you are. Be who you are. Express it with courage. Fearlessly, Ophelia. Without regrets. Bring who you are to life.

"Speak your truth. Speak loudly, whisper softly, but make your point. Whether people agree or disagree, whether it makes you popular or not. Say who you are. Be true to yourself. Know who you are and what you stand for—what you believe in, what you don't, what you'll tolerate and what you won't.

"If you need time, tell that truth about you. If you don't know, tell that truth about you. If you're not sure, say so. If you change your mind, let it be known. Say who you are. If you love someone, tell that truth. If you're angry, acknowledge it. If you disagree, admit it. Say who you are. Without need for approval. Without fear. Be who you are for the magnificent sake of being you.

"Be who you are, Ophelia.

"Do it with gusto. Live with gusto.

"Be true to yourself, be fearlessly honest—and everything around you will dance to that song. A fruit is not always ripe. That's okay. That's not the matter of it. Remember, my friend. *This* is the matter of it: be who you are, love who you are, and embrace the fact that you're worthy of every happiness you've ever imagined."

I opened my eyes and looked up into Gusto's. He smiled at me and said, "Do you understand?"

I nodded, pulled off the blanket, and stood up, facing the sun. The boat was rocking, but I felt completely steady. I held Gusto's hand, spread my arms, and got ready to fly.

33. The Secret to Flying

We flew. Soaring above the clouds and then diving down through them, feeling the mist against our faces. We joined the pelican that had given us a taste of flying days before and then broke off, just the two of us again, spiraling and circling.

"Do you want to know how to come back here?" Gusto said.

"Yes..." I never wanted to forget.

"Keep forgiving, Ophelia. Yourself. Others. Yourself again."

We pulled up through a thick cloud and rested on top of it. We sat there perched far above all that I knew, and Gusto said, "It's a decision, like everything else. But one that can be more difficult. That's why there's music."

I could feel it, the melody of forgiveness having worked its way through me.

"Yes, Ophelia. Oh the gift of it. And here you are now. I'll tell you something so that you remember. Next time you forget how to forgive or why you should forgive, stop doing whatever you're doing. It's that important. Stop right in the middle of it. Choose a song that pulls you toward it, the one that speaks to your emotions, whatever you're feeling.

"Play it loud enough so that you can think of nothing but the song itself. Play it until it takes you out of yourself and into the notes, the highs and lows. Let the music seep into you until all you can do is sway with it, be moved by it, feel it coursing through you.

"Play the music until something's changed inside of you, until you feel the shift, until you feel yourself as both the high notes and the low ones, as the union of all of them, and you realize that one can't exist without the other.

"Play it until the music speaks to you in the rhythms you need to hear, reminding you that you're learning. That you're *learning.* That it's okay. That you're good—and that good can come out of anything. *Anything,* Ophelia. Because even the most traumatic notes can reach up into something so different, changing their tone, becoming so breathlessly beautiful they move you to tears.

"Turn up the music. Play it until you know you are bound by nothing, supported by everything. Until you're no longer carrying the weight of blame or guilt or shame, until you've left them far behind, in the pile of lessons learned, freeing you to fly again.

"You see, no one can put your spark out. Only you can. But it doesn't do anyone any good. And it's your right not to. Indeed, my friend, it's your right to remember who you are and to let that be your compass as you move forward."

With that, Gusto took my hand, and we were off again. I didn't think about how to do it. I only thought about where we wanted to go, picturing us already there, imagining what that would feel like.

34. Living with Gusto

My husband and daughter were in the kitchen of the bungalow we were renting for three months. It was small and rustic and raw and colorful, and the three of us loved every inch of it. The music was playing on an old radio, words I didn't understand but that were sung with a passion that moved me, and I could hear the two of them laughing. They enjoyed cooking together now, using whatever ingredients were available, always at least one we had never heard of or tried. It was one of their many new hobbies.

By the time our daughter had finished her freshman year, my husband and I had sold our house, our second car, the majority of our photography equipment, our furniture, and our belongings that we no longer wanted to belong to. It wasn't sad, as so many people thought it was for us; it was liberating. We were doing it together. On my daughter's last day of classes, we packed up what now defined our life, drove to her school, picked her up, and kept on driving.

For a few days, we headed east, west, and south, back and forth, down. We stopped at a roadside café in Nevada to grab something to eat and looked at the map again. We discussed possibilities, where to go next, what we wanted to explore. Then my daughter closed the map of the States and said, "I have an idea. Let's cross the border." My husband and I looked at each other. "Let's go south," she said. "We could get a map of Baja, or maybe we don't even need one. We'll figure it. And I'll be your translator!" She had shown an unusual aptitude and keen interest in languages ever since doing a six-week exchange program in Marseille, France, her junior year of high school. She was proficient in French and Spanish.

There was nothing anticlimactic about crossing the border. As we left behind schedules and routines and old rules, as we left intended chaos and perfect order and more than plenty and advanced technology, as we left behind organization and structure and careful planning, as we traded cell phones for sunsets and store-bought for home-grown, as we entered a new landscape for us, stunning randomness, a usefulness for everything broken, simplicity in the complex, tradition revered, in that moment when the back wheels of the car were where we had been and the front wheels were leading us to where we were going, we held hands. The three of us.

After crossing the border in California, we drove down Baja for a few days, going back and forth from the Pacific side to the east side of the peninsula, eventually making our way down along the Sea of Cortez. We drove for hours without seeing any sign of civilization, coming upon inlets with white sand and turquoise water and a scattering of palapa shade umbrellas. We wondered who had constructed them and left them there for anyone to use. It made us feel welcomed by strangers. We stopped often, swimming at almost every beach that pulled to us as we neared it.

When we drove into the tiniest town I'd ever seen—two main dirt roads, one general store, and maybe twenty houses ranging from basic Baja luxury to raw cinder-block—my husband said it first. "I like it here." As I found out later, all three of us had the same feeling; we knew before we even got out of the car. We parked and walked down the narrow dirt road that led to the water. Old, weather-beaten houses lined each side, three on one side, four on the other. When we reached the beach, the tide was going out. We had to make our way over piles of river rocks to where the sand awaited us every time the water receded, following a gentle wave teasing the shore. As we carefully stepped over the rocks, my husband and I holding hands, I thought about all the hurdles we had crossed in the past few months to come back together. The opening up. The patience when a rock in front of us looked insurmountable. The relief as it fell to the size of a pebble through the act of forgiveness or the letting go of any agenda. The willingness to be vulnerable. The honesty. Seeing the obstacles for what they were, yet recognizing us as far more powerful. The sharing. The shifting of priorities. The importance of fun. Our map becoming question after question, the answers the keys to guide us. The listening. The talking. The sound of it all, that joining, like the water as it reached away from the sea, over the rocks, and then the *click-clack-click* as it pulled itself back into its home, the sea. My husband squeezed my hand.

To our right, an old man and a child were fishing from the shore. I followed the thread of their lines, trying to see how far out into the aqua water they had cast them. "Look at those colors," I said.

My daughter walked over to where they were, with my husband and I following. She asked the man if he would mind taking our picture. "The water," she said in Spanish, "it's beautiful." He smiled, took the camera, and then we thought maybe something was lost in translation because rather than taking the picture with the sea as the background, he kept repositioning himself every time we did, motioning for us to face the sea. Finally, we gave in. With his back to the sea, and us facing him, he took the picture. Still smiling, he handed the camera back to my daughter and then pointed at it, seeming to wait for something. "Gracias," my daughter said. But he kept standing there, smiling, pointing at the camera. After a short exchange, realizing Baja Spanish might be very different from the Spanish she was familiar with, my daughter said, "I think he wants us to look at the picture he took." So we did. We were in the picture, perfectly centered, but what drew my eye was the For Rent sign—in English—hanging on the screen door of the bungalow we had been standing in front of.

When we looked up from the camera display, the man had already joined the boy again.

We asked around and found the owner of the bungalow. It was a young woman, in her late twenties. I had never seen someone look so regal, such worldly eyes. A simple white dress, no makeup, her long, curly, black hair flowing freely. The house hadn't been rented in a long time, so she was happy to have us there, especially since we threw out the idea of maybe staying for three months. When she asked us if the price she had in mind would be okay with us, my husband and I looked at each other, a look that said, *That low? Is she kidding?* She wasn't. She was grateful but didn't seem surprised when my husband offered to fix the place up for her during our three months—since that time frame had somehow been decided—and she then made a point of telling us we could fix it up however we wanted to—that she liked us and trusted us and would be happy to have the house feel like us. There were no papers to sign, no deposits to make. We shook hands, punctuated by a nod, a slight bow to each other. We had known her for less than ten minutes.

Though we didn't see her often after that, we saw the old man and his grandson almost every day. The old man, who we soon called *Abuelo,* meaning Grandfather, taught my husband how to fish, and our daughter spent an hour or two a day playing with the grandson and teaching him English. I took a liking to the grandmother and visited her regularly. I helped *Abuela* tend her garden and encouraged her to relax in her rocking chair next to me as I dug my hands in the rich soil, trimmed stems and cut branches back, adjusted the tattered cloth shade as necessary, and watered the tomatoes, lettuce, parsley, chives, jalapenos, cilantro, beets, eggplant, carrots, basil, oregano, and the vegetables and spices I wasn't familiar with, whose names and tastes I had yet to learn. She was more than generous in sharing the almost daily harvest with us, but she didn't want us cooking for them. Not yet. She laughed and laughed as she explained why—in words I was totally fine with not understanding. God, I loved her laugh.

We were three weeks into our stay in a place filled with people who seemed to have been waiting for us to arrive. Except knowing that our daughter would eventually be going back to school, everything else was up in the air. Where we would go next. How we would make a steady income, whether or not we actually needed it to be steady. We were having a celebratory dinner, celebrating what the three of us had found together, celebrating the questions and possibilities for all that came next.

To the right of the kitchen, through a small doorway, was a three-walled sunroom. The fourth wall, steps away from the beach, was mostly screen. I took another step back to see the whole wall at once, the one opposite the screened wall. I had finally finished it. Painted words, notes to myself, numbered from one to twenty-six, covered the wall—except a three-square-foot space in the center. That's where I put the framed mirror I had made.

It was time. I could feel it.

The sun, low in the sky now, would be part of my reflection.

I reached down, picked up the thick bamboo ladder I had constructed and placed it against the wall. Only by climbing up those three rungs would I be able to fully see my face in the mirror.

I took one step up. And then the second. And then the third. And for the first time, I looked into the mirror I had created. And I listened.

* * *

Oh, Ophelia… it's more beautiful than the taste of the juiciest mango. Your ladder made of bamboo. So sturdy. So strong. You standing on it. Look at you—three feet off the ground. Not quite in the clouds, but higher than the ground. Yes! I love looking at you even up just that high, peering at yourself in your mirror. The frame. What creativity. And yes, I see all the details. The glass... what you've created with all those broken pieces. And the metal—those aren't scraps. Were they? I can't imagine... how you've pieced them all together into what it is now. And the stones in the corners, holding the frame together. Look at that! The sun is shining across the water, into the room, bouncing off the mirror, framing you within your frame, welcoming you once again to where you are. Well done.

And now. Now you want to breathe even more life into who you are. Of course. Are you really so surprised? You feel passion again, and that spark inside you has grown to a dancing flame. That's what happens when you remember the matter of it all.

As you watch your life continue to unfold before you, there's a question you'll wonder about. This is the answer to that question: No, Ophelia, it's not too good to be true. You created the magic with the thoughts you chose to think and the feelings you decided to feel. Don't question it or second-guess it or wonder if it's going to go away. It's not. It has no stopping point. It's not like Gusto's truck.

Keep being strong, Ophelia, because that's who you are. And now you know that the greatest strength—what takes the most courage—is to ask yourself, "Am I willing to love myself?" and to answer it with all the soul of who you are, "Yes. Without limits." And you see now what the universe orchestrates when the songs you give it to conduct come from that love.

How can I possibly thank you, Ophelia? I missed you so much. And now… look at you.

You remember who you are.

As you take more steps, more brilliant leaps into the richness of life, you're going to have an odd feeling that someone somewhere is dancing in celebration, watching you from an unseen distance with the most delicious delight. And every time you embrace that feeling, you'll let go of the trapeze you're swinging on—without any hesitation. Because you'll know that the next one is on its way, ready to arrive in your hands at the most timely moment. And you won't doubt for a second that there's always a net below. One you no longer need.

I smiled, realizing that I could no longer hear Gusto as someone separate from myself. He was in every thought I chose to think, each feeling I chose to feel, the words I chose to speak. I would no longer separate myself from me.

And yet, I had no doubt that the *someone somewhere watching my life unfold from an unseen distance* was Gusto. As seamless as we were, my Gusto was my audience. Always. Clapping and whistling between bites of mango.

My daughter and husband were standing in the doorway between the kitchen and sunroom as I stepped down the ladder. They were looking at me, smiling. Dinner was ready. The celebration was about to begin. I thought that's what they came to tell me. But it wasn't.

"Thank you, Mom," my daughter said.
"I see you, Ophelia," my husband said.

Notes to Myself

Don't give up. Instead, ask to be shown the way
when I need help. With anything.

Who I am is a decision I make, and I can change mood hats
whenever I want to. When in doubt, have fun…
and then decide.

I'm fun, and life is fun. If any thought I have suggests
otherwise, I'm going to let it go. I don't need it.

When I'm stuck, I can be my own ladder.
Honesty—first with myself, and then with other people—
brings me out of even the deepest of ruts and back to life.

I can change any part of my life I want to, whenever
I want to. But I'm not going to try to change who I am.
What I really want is to become more of who I am.

*When I look closely at what makes me happy
and what I'm grateful for, I can move on when it's time to—
from anything—without any bitterness, fully able to taste
the sweetness of what's next.*

*Being grateful isn't about staying where I am
in order to prove to myself that I'm thankful
for parts or even all of it. It's about being thankful
as I fill my life with more greatness.*

*Listen to the voice that calls to me. Always. Filled with
courage and wild trust, allow my heart to lead me.*

I have control over my life. I'm not a tennis ball.

I get to be responsible for my own happiness.

*I don't have to worry about whether or not I'll get what
I want because I can create what I want.*

*Every belief is a choice. I can change them, let go of them,
and create new ones. It's simple; just step out of my head
and into my heart. Feel what's true for me.*

*Until I hear a whisper or loud voice inside
telling me the next step, stand still
and let the how find its way to me.*

*When I feel moved to do something specific, I'll have my
full energy to do it. When that voice inside talks to me
or I feel a tiny push, I won't hesitate. I'll follow it.
In those inspired moments, every time I lift my foot,
I'll be bringing myself closer to what I want.*

*Along the way, remember to decide how I want to feel.
Set that intention deliberately, giving my attention
to the end, how I want to feel in the result—
and I'll take myself to that feeling.*

*It might just be that things are working out perfectly,
including the timing of things, better than I could even have
imagined. I'm going to wonder in that direction.
A lot.*

Fearlessly decide. And it will be so.

*No one but me can decide who I am,
what I'm capable of, and what my life should look like.
I'm embracing that honor.*

*I am Ophelia. That's the starting point of everything.
And the journey. And the destination.*

Love and let go. Freely. Generously.

Allow people to be who they are, noticing those rhythms that are harmonized with mine, sometimes a drumbeat, sometimes the whistle of a flute, bringing out music that wouldn't otherwise exist, and then eventually, there will be no one in my life who doesn't in some way or another encourage me to sing.

I trust myself to remember who I am. Always. I have it in me.

When in the midst of making a change, there's excitement in the unknowns and uncertainties.

I trust myself.

I trust my life.

I'm worthy of every happiness I've ever imagined— always. End of sentence.

If you enjoyed *Living with Gusto,*
please consider posting a review at Amazon.com
or elsewhere online.

Thank you!

You're Invited

Hang out with Gusto at TheGustoCafe.com.

TheGustoCafe.com is open 24/7, with the exact love note you need, whenever you need it—because you're awesome, and it's important to remember that.

Explore the café and find powerful Relationship Reminders, helpful Timing Tips, and daily Power Thoughts. Read a page in the Empowerment Diary and feel your confidence soar. Get encouraged and excited by reading a Note to You from Your Future Self. Listen to music and read a short, moving Love Story. Get advice about how to interact with money and learn how to live your dream—today, right now. Post your thoughts and be heard. Click on the ladder in the café and climb out of any rut. Click on the wall art in the café and get inspired to fall even more in love with your life.

Get wildly empowered.

Hang out with Gusto at TheGustoCafe.com.